MW01148792

ALEXA WEST GUIDES

South Korea

The Solo Girl's Travel Guide updates this guidebook year-round as businesses grow, change, and even sometimes, close. If you notice a change we should know about, please let us know at hello@thesologirlstravelguide. com so we can update our guide for future travelers!

STOCK OUR BOOK

Want to stock our book in your shop, store or platform? Send us a message at hello@thesologirlstravelguide.com

TRAVEL WITH INTEGRITY

It feels good to support the people and places in this book.

We are about to introduce you to good people, good places and good businesses that deserve your time.

the SOLO GIRL'S TRAVEL GUIDE

SOUTH KOREA

ALEXA WEST GUIDES

The Solo Girl's Travel Guide Mantra

"THE BEST ADVENTURES START WITH THE SIMPLE DECISION TO GO."

Every girl should travel solo at least once in her life.

You don't need a boyfriend, a travel partner or anyone's approval to travel the world. And you don't need a massive bank account or an entire summer off work.

All you need is that wanderlust in your blood and a good guide book in your hands.

If you've doubted yourself for one moment, remember this:

Millions of girls travel across the globe all by themselves every damn day and you can, too.

You are just as capable, just as smart, and just as brave as the rest of us. You don't need permission - this is your life.

Listen to your gut, follow your heart, and just book that ticket already!

A QUICK NOTE ABOUT THIS BOOK.

This South Korea Guide Book is different from all the other guidebooks I've ever written. It's different because of one thing: Korean culture.

Korean culture is particular, it's rich, it's beautiful, it's puzzling. It's this culture that makes Korea an unforgettable experience that will be stamped upon your soul, but it's also this culture that requires a bit of studying before you come in order to feel like you can truly begin to unlock the many layers of this beautifully dynamic country.

While this book is, of course, an incredible guide to help you seamlessly plan your Korean adventure, it is also so heavily a culture guide. Understand Korean day-to-day culture with its unstated intricacies and you will be able to instantly dive below the tourist surface. And that is what you're about to do.

I have enjoyed writing about the delicate and sharp Korean traditions and culture in this book so much that I know you're going to love devouring it, too.

Enjoy, *chingu.*

Pssst, hey you!

Want this pretty book on your phone?
Get the digital guide here.

WHAT READERS
ARE SAYING...

"I could not put it down and was so intrigued by all the pro tips and fun facts - I learned so much! I absolutely love the travel community this book brought me to as well. This guide book will give you *very* helpful tips, detailed transportation guides, informative explanations of activities and lodgings, honest reviews of various places, and the confidence boost you didn't know you needed. Would definitely recommend this book to other travelers or even just South Korea enthusiasts."

-Heather

"I've been interested in traveling to/applying to work in Korea for a while now, but I wanted someone to explain the ins-and-outs of being a single woman in a foreign country. I appreciate Alexa's candor and how she takes women's safety & comfort into consideration before recommending a place. Definitely makes me feel at ease!"

-Hannah

MORE REVIEWS COMING SOON.
(HOPEFULLY THAT'S YOU)

The 7 Travel Commandments

BY THE SOLO GIRL'S TRAVEL GUIDE

01 BE A TRAVELER, NOT A TOURIST.

Don't go through your trip (and life) on the shallow end. Dive deep. Put your phone down. Be present.

02 TRAVEL SLOWLY

Count experiences, not passport stamps.

03 TRAVEL ECO

Bring your own water bottle, canvas bag, and reusable straw to help you avoid single-use plastics.

04 MIND YOUR IMPACT

Leave every place better than you found it. Take a piece of trash from the beach and be kind to people you meet.

05 VOTE WITH YOUR DOLLAR

When possible, choose to support local businesses, eat locally sourced food, join tour companies that operate ethically (aka don't work with animals, respect the environment, benefit their local communities) and/or businesses that just treat their staff really really well.

06 TRUST YOUR GUT

Listen to that little voice inside you. When something doesn't feel right, back away. When something feels good, lean. Your intuition will lead you to beautiful places, unforgettable moments, and new lifelong friends.

07 CARRY YOUR POSITIVITY

Ever had a crappy day and then a stranger smiles at you and flips your entire mood? Travel can be hard, but your positivity will be your secret weapon. Happy vibes are contagious. Even when we don't speak the local language, a smile or a random act of kindness tips the universal scale in the right direction for you and the people you meet along your journey.

It feels good to support the people and places in this book.
We are about to introduce you to good people, good places and good businesses that deserve your time.

Hi! I'm Alexa...

Back in 2010, I was a broke-ass Seattle girl who had just graduated from college and had about $200 to my name. I was faced with two choices: get a job, a husband, and have 3 babies plus a mortgage...or sell everything I owned and travel the world.

Obviously, I made the right choice.

For the past 10 years, I've been traveling the world solo, including two years of living in South Korea as an English teacher and full-time foodie. As I've traveled, I've played every travel role from being the young volunteer and broke backpacker to flying to exotic islands to review new luxury hotels and give breath to struggling tourism industries.

Now I spend my days as an explorer on a mission to change the way that women travel the world. I want to show you places you've never seen and unlock hidden doors you never knew existed in places you may have been before. I want to create a path for you where you feel safe while diving deeper into cultures and countries beyond your own – whether for a week, a year, or a lifetime. And that's what I'm doing.

As the creator of The Solo Girl's Travel Guide, I can write whatever the hell I want. I want to write about things that matter and adventures that change you. So, follow in my footsteps and let's do this together.

xoxo, Alexa

Don't forget your map!

TO KEEP THE PRICE OF THIS BOOK AFFORDABLE FOR YOU, THERE ARE NO FANCY COLOR MAPS INSIDE.

I'VE GOT SOMETHING EVEN BETTER.

VISIT THE LINK BELOW TO GET YOUR INTERACTIVE SOUTH KOREA MAP THAT YOU CAN TRAVEL WITH.

A little bit of honesty...

I'm not here to get rich or reach 1 million followers on Instagram.

I'm here because I love to travel. And I love to help other girls travel, too. Simple as that.

I started writing The Solo Girl's Travel Guide for my actual friends planning big trips around the world.

All with the goal of showing them how to travel in a short amount of time on a realistic budget. And now, I write this book for you.

So! A true South Korea vacation should be equal amounts of street food, temple hopping, and nightlife. And that's exactly what this guide is.

What this Guide is not . . .

✗ An overwhelming deep-dive into South Korea's history

✗ An 8-hour read with historical dates and ancient facts

✗ A book written by some man who just doesn't get it . . .

Speaking of men, since the success of The Solo Girl's Travel Guide, I've had many dudes ask me, "Yeah, but why a girl's guide?"

Um, because we have breasts. And for some reason, that's enough for the world to treat us like toys. We constantly have to ask ourselves questions like . . .

→ Are there drugs in my drink?

→ Is that dark alley filled with serial killers?

→ Am I going to be kidnapped and sold to the highest bidder?

The answer is usually no, but for us girls, "usually" doesn't cut it. In order to be wild and carefree, we've got to feel 100% safe. And I've never found a travel guide to take my safety into consideration . . . so, here we are.

Go into your vacation knowing that I'm leading you to the best, the safest, and the totally worth it spots. Let your hair down and tell your mom not to worry. I've got you.

So, as we get into this guide—I want to make a few promises to you:

→ I won't bullshit you and tell you that a hotel is awesome if it's not.

→ I will tell you what spots are worth your time—and what spots to skip.

→ And I will make planning this vacation so easy and so fun!!!

Your bags may not be packed, but your vacation officially starts now.

Oh, and once you've bought this book . . . we're officially friends. I'm here if you need me. Just write me on Instagram @SoloGirlsTravelGuide

FLIGHTS, AIRPORTS, WALKING AROUND TOWN...

TRAVEL IS A LITTLE BIT MORE MAGICAL WHEN GOOD MUSIC IS INVOLVED.

FIND MY SOUTH KOREA PLAYLIST HERE.

LET'S GO TO SOUTH KOREA!

THIS BOOK IS YOUR SHORTCUT TO AN AMAZING KOREA ADVENTURE.

You ready?

TRAVEL FAR ENOUGH TO MEET YOURSELF.

South Korea

TABLE OF CONTENTS

are you ready? let's do this!

SEE A GIRL TRAVELING WITH THIS GEAR?

SAY HI.

SHE'S YOUR SISTER IN THE

Solo Girl's Travel Club

CARRY THIS GEAR
AS AN INVITATION TO FRIENDSHIP

GET IT HERE

OR AT ALEXA-WEST.COM

INTRODUCTION TO

South Korea

INTRODUCTION TO

South Korea

We're going to make this quick.

South Korea's history is one of kingdoms and invasions, wars, and oppression.

The Korean peninsula was inhabited by Siberians and Mongolians as early as the 4th century BCE. With time, settlements and groups merged into one unified kingdom. Chinese invasions caused the peninsula's first partition, breaking it down to three kingdoms until 901 A.D. when it was unified again by a powerful noble who gave it the name Koryo (that's where Korea's western name comes from).

After invasions from the Japanese and the Manchus between the 16th and 17th centuries, Korea decided to seclude itself from the outside world. A very long period of peace followed...but Korea remained isolated from the developing world until the 19th Century when European countries started pressing Korea to open up in hopes of developing trade and diplomatic relations. Korea refused and invasions followed. As the 20th century began, Japan, China, and Russia tried to seize control of the peninsula. Japan succeeded.

Japanese occupancy began in 1905 and for the next 35 years, Korea became a developing and industrialized country but at the hands of brutal repression by the Japanese. As their colony, Japan aimed to erase Korea's identity to merge it with their own.

WWII brought Japan's defeat and a big change for Korea when the United States and the Soviet Union partitioned the peninsula into two. The Northern half stayed under the Soviet's "supervision" and became the Democratic People's Republic of Korea (DPRK) while the southern half remained under the influence of the United States who installed a strongly anti-communist goverment in its new capital: Seoul.

In 1950, the communists in the north invaded South Korea, sparking the Korean War, which lasted 3 years and cost more than 2.5 million lives of Koreans, Americans, and Chinese. The war was never officially over and still today, the two Koreas remain divided in a somewhat permanent climate of tension.

Today, South Korea is a mixture between tradition and innovation between cultural legacy, and high technological development. Its history of oppression turned it into a resilient country that is now one of the biggest economies in Eastern Asia. And into one of the friendliest with some of the kindest people I've ever encountered.

Got all that? Okay, let's keep going...

SOUTH KOREA 101

———

LANGUAGE: Korean (Hangul)

POPULATION: 52 million (not including the foreign expats, students and teachers)

TOTAL AREA: 38,691 mi²

CURRENCY: Korean Won (KRW)

TIME ZONE: GMT+9

RELIGION: Buddhist, Christian, Non-Practicing

———

THE FOOD

Korean food has a lot of history. Kimchi is fermented by burying it in the ground, an ancient practice that allowed Koreans to enjoy fresh(ish) vegetables during the winter. Spam (yes, spam from the can) became popular during the Korean War via American influence. And so on. You can find a lot of history in Korean food today, but you'll also find a lot of modernity. You can eat traditionally every night of the week or go for a big juicy burger. The options are forever endless. Oh and heads up: The chopsticks in Korea are typically metal with a sort of flat shape so…good luck with that. If you can master them, I salute you.

THE RELIGION

Historically, South Korea has practiced Buddhism. You'll see opulent Buddhist temples all over the country and while Korean people may participate in ceremonies or include religion in traditional events with a religious undertone, a large percentage of Korean people have drifted from Buddhism. About half of Korea's population are non-religious, while the other half are split between Buddhism or Christianity in some form or another.

THE PEOPLE

Positive. You will have a positive experience with Koreans who believe in respect above all else...as long as you maintain and return the respect back, understandably so. To understand what I'm about to say next, it's helpful to realize that the American military has been present in Korea for decades, and to this day, has multiple American military bases around the country. In addition to that, nowadays, Korea employs thousands of English-speakers to teach their youth. So there is a huge American/foreign presence in Korea - a country that is otherwise homogeneous. Some Koreans welcome this foreign presence (especially those in tourism and education) but some Koreans are over it. With that being said, I have encountered both attitudes from people in Korea: welcoming and unwelcoming. I've met Koreans that are so warm and hospitable that they'll invite you over to their house to eat dinner with their family and I've also met Koreans that see waygookin (foreigners) as a nuisance.

To have a good experience with Korean people, just behave. Don't be a crazy person on spring break. Be polite. And you will likely be met with kindness and warmth.

Ps. At the end of this book, I'll share a few stories about some of my interactions with Korean strangers throughout the country...

THE CRIME

Korea is so freaking safe! There was never a day that I felt unsafe walking alone or living alone. Korea is so safe that I once saw two men get in a fight with their hands self-secured behind their backs while they shoulder-butted each other because, even in an altercation, they were following the strict laws against hitting someone else. The biggest crimes in South Korea are phone theft (watch your phone at the bars), drunk driving and domestic abuse between couples...I'm not kidding when I say that couples have been so desensitized by Korean Dramas that they scream, cry, and even slap each other more normally than what is healthy.

THE VOLTAGE

South Korea uses 220 voltage (as opposed to the standard 110v used in the U.S.). In other words, your curling iron and hair dryer won't survive. Don't bring them.

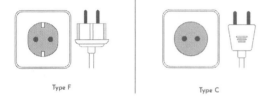

Type F   Type C

THE WEATHER

South Korea has all four seasons! The weather patterns vary quite a bit season to season but with the right preparation (right here, girl!), you'll be covered for anything.

Mainland Korea experiences colder weather from November through March and warmer temperatures April-October. Jeju Island is in a sub-tropical zone and stays about 10-15 degrees warmer than the mainland, making it a popular winter vacation spot all year round.

Here's a quick guide to weather in South Korea...

 High Season (Popular Season): June-August and late January to mid-February (depending on when the Korean Lunar New Year falls) are incredibly popular travel periods among Koreans themselves, with the prices to match.

Low Season: Winter months, November-February. Expect fewer tourists and cheaper prices.

Rainy Season: Late June to mid-July. You can expect bursts of heavy rain rather than all-day rainy weather.

Hottest Months: July-August

Coldest Months: December-February

Official Best Times to Visit South Korea: Spring and fall

Alexa's Vote for Best Time to Visit: I agree with the hype...spring and fall are the best times to visit South Korea in terms of both ideal travel weather and fewer domestic crowds, but I love South Korea year-round! If you're not turned off by heat and humidity or by cold temperatures, the country has some incredible festivals and other things to experience in the summer and winter.

A DEEPER DIVE INTO KOREAN WEATHER AND WHAT TO EXPECT

◊**Spring:** *March-May*

Spring in Korea is lovely! The temperatures are mild, averaging around mid-60 degrees Fahrenheit (15-20 degrees Celsius). You might get a few rainy days but spring is generally pretty dry in South Korea.

Best For: This is the time of year to catch the plum and cherry blossoms! That's right, it's not just Japan that has cherry blossoms! One thing to watch out for, though, is Korea's famous yellow dust, which blows in from Mongolia and the Gobi Desert during the spring. Feel free to wear a face mask like the locals on days when the dust level is particularly high, or entertain yourself indoors with Korea's plethora of shopping and museums! This sounds scary...but I promise it's not. #TheMoreYouKnow

◊**Summer:** *June-August*

Get ready for hot and humid! Temperatures hover around 85 degrees Fahrenheit (29 degrees Celsius) and humidity levels can reach up to 80 percent! So don't even think of bringing a curling iron. The rainy season happens late June to mid-July and can bring exciting torrential downpours. They typically last just a couple hours per day!

Best For: Heading to the beach in Busan, exploring the waters near Yeonsong or spending all day outside exploring Seoul.

◊ **Autumn:** *September-November*

Autumn in Korea is gorgeous and cozy with comfortable temperatures around 65-68 degrees Fahrenheit (18-20 degrees Celsius). The rainy season typically ends at the beginning of fall, making for dry, sunny days and cool nights. Seasonal winds can bring the yellow dust back in the fall but it's typically lighter than in the spring.

Best For: Korea's beautiful fall foliage! Fall is my favorite season to go hiking in South Korea!

◊ **Winter:** *November-March*

Winter in Korea requires a really warm coat and a scarf! Winter is South Korea's longest season and is cold and dry. Thank goodness it's dry! Temperatures can get down to about 20 degrees Fahrenheit (-6 degrees Celsius), particularly in the northern parts of the country. The northern areas also tend to see more snow.

Best For: Museums, Korea's cafe culture, drinking Soju and enjoying less tourists!

Conclusion, pack accordingly! South Korea's seasons are quintessential to their reputation.

Speaking of packing...check out my Korean Packing List on page 254 or go here for the fancy version:

A MENTAL MAP OF
South Korea

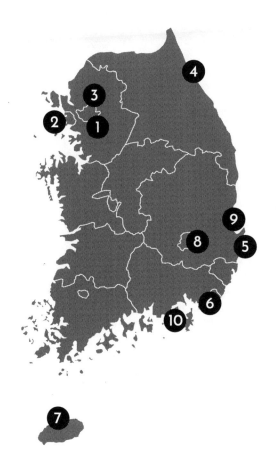

SEOUL	**1**	**6**	BUSAN	
INCHEON	**2**	**7**	JEJU ISLAND	
DMZ	**3**	**8**	DAEGU	
GANGNEUNG	**4**	**9**	POHANG	
GYEONGJU	**5**	**10**	GEOJE, TONGYEONG & THE SOUTHERN TIP	

AREAS TO KNOW
in South Korea

SEOUL

The heart of South Korea, Seoul is the city of endless possibilities. Connected by an extremely efficient subway system, it's easy to get from one side of the city to the next. Jump from K-Pop shopping districts to the western nightlife area or go from the business district to the red-light district in 30 minutes. A city with a population of almost 10 million, Seoul is the place to immerse yourself in everything that South Korea has to offer.

INCHEON

You might find yourself flying into Incheon airport. Incheon is actually an island 30 minutes northwest of Seoul where...not a lot is happening for vacationers. That's not to say, however, that Incheon isn't worth a visit. It just isn't at the top of my "must see" list if you've only got 30 days to explore.

For this reason, I will give you an Incheon Bucket List later in this book, rather than a full chapter. If you do decide to visit Incheon, I recommend sleeping in Seoul and making Inchon your day trip.

DMZ

For a once-in-a-lifetime glimpse into one of the most mysterious places on earth, head about an hour north from Seoul to the DMZ (demilitarized zone), the stretch of land that acts as a buffer between North and South Korea. This area is best explored with an organized tour. I recommend this one ☞

GANGNEUNG

From Seoul, head east to the coast where you'll find Gangneung, a city of festivals and beaches. Life is slow here except when there is a coffee festival, a film festival or the famous Gangneung Danoje Festival. Gangneung is home to the largest beach on the east coast called Gyeongpo Beach. In the spring, this beach is lined with blossoming cherry blossoms and in the winter, Gangneung isn't a stranger to snow!

GYEONGJU

Continue south as you hug the coast until you reach Gyeongju. Often referred to as South Korea's "museum without walls," this city is filled with culture, history, and fascinating archaeological sites. The other main reason to visit Gyeongju: The Jungang Night Market.

BUSAN

Busan is the "Miami Beach" of South Korea but with less skin. You'll find yourself hanging out on the sandy beaches of Gwangju or Haeundae where beach bars and sky rise bars are packed every night of the week. You'll find great fish markets, fresh seafood, and tons of BBQ joints. There are also a plethora of Jjimjilbangs (spas) in Busan.

This city is where old meets- explore old school neighborhoods one minute then step into lavish department stores the next. The only downfall is that Busan gets crowded with tourists during the summer. As one of the most popular locations for ESL teachers, you can also expect a big party scene with expats from all over the world.

JEJU ISLAND

Often called "the Hawaii of South Korea", Jeju Island is a nice break from city life. Stunning waterfalls, soft sand beaches, and opulent hotels make Jeju the perfect spot to kick your feet up with an umbrella drink or two. If you know how to ride a scooter, rent one and explore the island. To get here, there are flights and ferries to the mainland every day!

DAEGU

A city that I didn't write a full chapter on...but is my #1 vote for teachers. The expat community in Daegu is incredibly close with theater troops, softball beer leagues, dance studios and hiking trails. The food is incredible, the shopping is top notch and the location is off the beaten path...despite being the 4th biggest city in the country. If you're considering teaching in Korea, check out Daegu.

POHANG

A small community of just 500,000, Pohang is an easy city to settle into. Located on the coast, you've got a beach to play volleyball on in the summer, a softball league to join in the spring, and temperate weather that won't make you freeze to death in the winter. You'll find hiking trails and waterfalls not too far, Busan is just a bus ride away, and local prices are very reasonable. If you're looking for a laid-back, intimate experience in South Korea, go to Pohang.

GEOJE, TONGYEONG AND THE SOUTHERN TIP

If you look on a map, The southeastern region of South Korea looks impossible to trace with a bazillion coves, islands, rivers, and inlets. Down here, you can play on the water, go deep sea fishing, camp on the beach, and wander through local villages. Again, these areas are small so instead of full chapters, later in this book I'll point you in the direction of places to stay and things to do. The rest is 100% a spontaneous adventure.

Fun Fact! South Korea has more than 3,000 islands, and it would take you an estimated 9 years to visit them all.

THE MINI
South Korea
BUCKET LIST

TOP 10 EXPERIENCES IN SOUTH KOREA

01 Go to a Jjimjilbang for a Korean body scrub

02 Sleep in a jjimjilbang!

03 Attend a K-pop Concert

04 Eat Korean BBQ

05 Visit the DMZ

06 Go on a Food Tour

07 Eat at a night market

08 Sing in a Noraebang

09 Ride the Subway in Seoul

10 Spend the night at a Buddhist temple

Bonus! Attend a Baseball Game (it's a whole new experience)

TOP 10 SOUTH KOREAN TEMPLES AND PALACES

Korea is mostly a Buddhist country, with Christianity following behind. These temples not only represent religion, but they represent Korea's deep history that intertwines with neighboring Asian countries and cultures. Keep an eye out for the overlap.

01 Gyeongbokgung Palace – *Seoul*

02 Haedong Yonggungsa Temple - *Busan*

03 Sanbang Temple & Grotto - *Jeju Island*

04 Suguksa Temple - *Seoul*

05 Seokbulsa Temple - *Busan*

06 Jingwansa Temple - *Seoul*

07 Changdeokgung & Changgyeonggung (East Palace complex) - *Seoul*

08 Busanjinjiseong (Jaseongdae Japanese Castle) - *Busan*

09 Gyeongju Eupseong Fortress - *Gyeongju*

10 Geumjeongsanseong Fortress – *Busan*

TOP 10 HIKES IN SOUTH KOREA

Korea has a huge hiking culture, so much so, that Korean hiking fashion is a huge deal and Koreans will spend hundreds of dollars on their outdoor outfits.

01 Seoraksan – *Seoul*

02 Hallasan - *Jeju Island*

03 Bukhansan - *Seoul*

04 Igidae Park - *Busan*

05 Geumnyeongsan Mountain - *Busan*

06 Seunghaksan Mountain - *Busan*

07 Mt. Namsan - *Gyeongju*

08 Achasan - *Seoul*

09 Dobongsan – *Seoul*

10 Jeongdong-Simgok Badabuchae-gil Trail - *Gangneung*

TOP 10 SOUTH KOREAN MARKETS

From fanny packs to fish, you can find just about anything in a South Korean market...

01 Namdaemun Market – *Seoul*

02 Jagalchi Fish Market – *Busan*

03 Noryangjin Fish Market - *Seoul*

04 Seoul Folk Flea Market - *Seoul*

05 Dongdaemun Market – *Seoul*

06 Gukje Market - *Busan*

07 Gwangjang Market - *Seoul*

08 Seogwipo Maeil Olle Market - *Jeju Island*

09 Jungang Market - *Gangneung*

10 Seongdong Market - *Gyeongju*

TOP 5 SOUTH KOREAN BEAUTY TRENDS

01 Sheet Masks

02 Eyelash Extensions

03 Body scrub in a Jjimjilbang

04 Tinted eyebrows from Etude House

05 Snail mucus

BEST PLACES TO SHOP FOR SKINCARE PRODUCTS AND COSMETICS COUNTRYWIDE

☆ Etude House

☆ Innisfree (my FAV because you'll also walk away with loads of free samples every time)

☆ Aritaum

☆ Olive Young

Beauty Notes...

....

....

....

....

....

BEAUTY TRENDS YOU CAN FEEL OKAY SKIPPING

Colored Eye Contacts

The way it's been explained to me by my Korean girlfriends is that everyone has the same color eyes in Korea so popping in green, blue or purple contacts is a fun way to mix things up. BUT these contacts can damage your eyeballs and your vision over time. This is a trend that I recommend avoiding.

Skin Bleaching

To a lot of South Koreans (and in Asian culture in general), lighter skin is considered more beautiful. Why? Because in Asia, darker skin is a sign that you work in the sun like a laborer or a farmer; whereas white skin means that you work inside, in an office and thus are more educated and more wealthy.

This has led to a multi-billion dollar skin whitening (read: bleaching) industry. From creams to pills, skin whitening is big business! You'll see these products advertised on billboards and in subways, and cosmetic shops and pharmacies will have rows upon rows of them. Even Chanel makes versions of their most popular foundations with skin whitening - just to sell in Asia

Just go ahead and skip this particular trend — not only is these products' effectiveness questionable, but because they contain harsh chemicals that can potentially cause lasting damage to your skin.

Fun Fact!

South Korea is one of the most notorious makeup and cosmetic capitals in the world. And men use makeup and beauty products as much as women.

South Korea Survival Guide

THIS SECTION IS FULL OF SHORTCUTS TO FAST TRACK
YOU TO EXPERIENCING KOREA AS A TRAVELER,
NOT A TOURIST.

———

ARRIVING IN KOREA

Visas for Korea

You've got options, chingu.

(chingu means friend in Korean)

THE TOURIST VISA

Great news - South Korea doesn't require a tourist visa for travelers from many countries!

Here's a shortlist of countries that don't need a visa for touring South Korea:

◇**United States** - (stay up to 90 days)

◇**Canada** - (visit up to 180 days)

◇**Australia** - (visit up to 30 days)

◇**New Zealand** - (visit up to 90 days)

◇**United Kingdom** - (visit up to 90 days)

◇**Ireland** - (visit up to 90 days)

◇**South Africa** - (visit up to 30 days)

If your country isn't listed above, go here for the full list!

Here's what you need to come to Korea on a Tourist Visa:

→ A valid passport with at least 2 blank pages in your passport

→ A negative COVID test at least 72 hours before you land in South Korea

→ Apply for your Korea Electronic Travel Authorization (K-ETA) 24 hours before you fly. It will cost 10,000 KRW or a little less than $9 USD.

→ This is basically just a form with all your information on it. **Note:** They will ask for your "address" in Korea. Just put your hotel address.

Note: They will ask for your "purpose of travel" which is likely "tourism".

Apply here:

THE WORKING HOLIDAY VISA

Want to stay in South Korea for up to one year while you travel, study or live the digital nomad life? Apply for the Working Holiday Visa!

Here are the basic requirements:

Australia	Austria	Belgium
Canada	Chile	Czech Republic
Denmark	France	Germany
Hong Kong	Hungary	Ireland
Israel	Italy	Japan
Netherlands	New Zealand	Poland
Portugal	Spain	Poland
Taiwan	U.K.	U.S.A.

2. Be between the ages of 18 to 30 years old

3. Prove you have sufficient funds to cover your trip, in this case its 3,000,000 KRW or roughly $2,500 USD in your bank account

4. Have a clean criminal record

Note! You can only apply for this visa once! Use it to the fullest!

THE TEACHER'S VISA

...it's actually called a Working Visa. If you are coming to teach English in South Korea, then you already have a school lined up that will apply for your visa for you and walk you through your collection of documents. On this visa, you can stay in South Korea for one year.

Note! The process from applying for a teaching position to actually flying to South Korea can be up to eight months, so if you're considering this option - you can start job hunting now.

For my FULL GUIDE on teaching English in South Korea, go here...

Ps. Teaching English in South Korea were some of the best years of my life! I highly recommend it!

KOREAN CULTURE, FOOD & ETIQUETTE

Korea is a country bound by culture, respect and tradition. When I moved to Korea, I wish I had this guide...it would have helped me avoid so many awkward situations and possibly rude behaviors.

Let's start with the heart and soul of Korean culture: food.

Korean Restaurant Culture 101

Tables usually have buzzers on them to call the staff to you. If not, you must shout (yes, shout across the room) 'Yogiyo' to get the attention of the staff. Sometimes, wonderfully so, the entire staff in the restaurant will respond in unison with a "NE!" which means, "yes" or "yes, we heard you, coming!". This will feel super rude in the beginning until you watch locals doing it around you and then you'll eventually get the courage to yogigo yourself.

Must-Try Korean Food & Drinks

WHAT TO EAT

I still dream about South Korea's rich stews, spicy meat, fresh-off-the-boat seafood, and unique sweets! Here are the Korean staples to try!

BIBIMBAP

Warm rice topped with kimchi, ground beef, veggies, spicy sauce, and a fried egg. The ultimate comfort food. Bibimbap is probably the most well-known Korean dish, other than Korean BBQ, but don't turn your nose up at it just because you've had it before! I promise, there is nothing like authentic bibimbap served up by a South Korean ajumma.

Speaking of bibimbap . . . try the dolsot variety!

Dolsot Bibimbap is my preferred way to eat bibimbap. The dish comes served in a sizzling hot stone pot, which gives the rice at the bottom a delightfully crispy texture and toasted taste. You can stir the egg around and it becomes more cooked inside the dish.

KIMCHI

Fermented vegetables (most often cabbage or daikon radish) seasoned with a range of spicy and sour flavors. Let's just be honest, though: there is good kimchi and there is bad kimchi. If you don't love it the first time, don't be afraid to try it again! You'll have plenty of opportunity - it's served with nearly every meal.

BANCHAN

The endless stream of complimentary side dishes that come with most every South Korean meal are called "banchan". These small plates will often include kimchi, seasoned spinach, seasoned bean sprouts, stir-fried eggplant, and potato salad.

BULGOGI

Grilled marinated beef, often grilled with onions and garlic and served with lettuce wraps and ssamjang, a thick spicy sauce.

SAMGYEOPSAL

Slices of grilled pork belly; dip them in sesame seasoning and eat them in lettuce wraps with grilled garlic and onion and of course, kimchi.

JAPCHAE

Stir-fried sweet potato noodles, often served with shredded veggies or beef. The noodles have a slightly sweet taste and a unique chewy texture.

TTEOKBOKKI

Chewy, sausage-shaped rice cakes topped with a sweet and spicy red chili paste. This is a very common street food item! You'll see people walking around eating them out of a cup with a little pokey stick instead of a fork.

SUNDUBU-JJIGAE

This heavenly dish consists of spicy tofu stew with veggies and seafood (sometimes beef or pork). It's served boiling hot and you are given a raw egg to crack into the broth. The egg poaches in the hot liquid, giving the soup a rich, creamy texture.

PAJEON

Savory pancakes of flour, eggs, and green onions. Pajeon comes with a wide variety of ingredients, including vegetables and seafood.

SAMGYETANG

Rich chicken and ginseng soup touted for its nutritional value and immune-boosting benefits. This dish is most commonly served in the summer months; Korean traditional beliefs have it that the nutritious broth helps replenish the body's minerals lost due to sweating.

SUNDAE

Korean blood sausage: chewy on the outside, soft and flavorful on the inside. Maybe not for the faint of heart, but if you're up for some adventure, it's actually delicious!

NAENGMYEON

Cold buckwheat noodles served with thin sliced beef, vegetables, and a hard-boiled egg. Super refreshing in the hot summer months!

HOTTEOK

A combination of pancake and fried dough, this delicious street food is filled with cinnamon, honey, brown sugar, and peanuts. The street food vendors will fry it up fresh on a griddle so you can eat it piping hot.

KOREAN FRIED CHICKEN

You might be thinking, "Why would I go all the way to South Korea and eat fried chicken?" But hear me out. Korean fried chicken is crispy and juicy, and comes in an almost endless variety of sauces and seasonings. Paired with an ice-cold beer, it's absolute perfection!

DOENJANG JJIGAE

Creamy, savory soybean paste stew. This often comes as a side dish with Korean BBQ.

KIMBAP

Known as Korean sushi, gimbap (kimbap) is rice, vegetables, strips of egg omelet, and sometimes meat, all wrapped up in a seaweed roll. Great for a quick on-the-go lunch!

What's inside the kimbap varies. Here are some types to try:

→ Canned Tuna Kimbap (my favorite): Chamchi kimbap

→ Vegetarian Kimbap: Yachae Kimbap

→ Beef Kimbap: Sogogi Kimbap

→ Egg Kimbap: Gyelan kimbap

DAK GALBI

Spicy stir-fried chicken and vegetables, often served topped with a pile of melty cheese. Trust me - always order it with the cheese!

GALBI JJIM

Braised short ribs (beef or pork) in a rich, succulent sauce.

HAEJANGGUK

Classic hangover stew! This can include beef or pork, vegetables, and dried Napa cabbage in a rich, hearty broth.

GAMJA-TANG

Spicy pork backbone stew with potatoes, cellophane noodles, and vegetables.

EOMUK BOKKEUM

Stir-fried fish cakes. These chewy treats have a pungent flavor and are often served as side dishes; you'll also see them a lot as street food.

NAKJI

Octopus! You can get it stir-fried in spicy sauce (nakji-bokkeum) or if you're feeling daring, you can eat it raw and still wriggling (san-nakji). If you go for the latter option, you'll need to coat it in sesame oil before you eat it to keep the suckers from sticking to your mouth! (Okay, maybe this one isn't a must-try . . .)

BINGSU

This unique shaved ice dessert comes topped with fruit, jam, syrup, and other sweet treats. For a really Korean version, try patbingsu - a sweet red bean flavor!

SSAMJANG

A spicy red sauce that is often served with Korean BBQ and is best paired with meat

Fun Fact! Seaweed soup is a common birthday dish.

WHAT TO DRINK

SOJU

See those bright green glass bottles? That's soju, the #1 sold and consumed alcohol in the whole entire country. It's cheap and it's easy to drink. What is it? It's a spirit distilled from starchy produce, usually grains. I've always said that it tastes like stale lemon water mixed with vodka. A few shots of soju won't hurt...but soju is so easy to drink that, before you know it, you've drunk an entire bottle and are blacked out at dinner. Soju is often drunk straight but you can mix it with water...or beer.

◊ **Soju Drinking Game:** The soju cap, when twisted off, comes with a little tail. Twirl it up and pass it around the table. Each person flicks the tail. Whoever flicks it to breaking point, the person to their right has to take a shot or drink.

◊ **Soju Drinking Game #2:** The inside of a Soju cap has a number. One person knows the number, the others go around the table guessing the number. Whoever guesses closest has to take a shot.

MEKJU

Beer. Korean beer is often light. Think Coors Light. There are lots of options to choose from like Hite (pronounced Hi-tuh) or Cass (pronounced Cass-uh). I love Korea because sometimes, depending on the mini mart, you may only be able to buy beer in 1-liter plastic bottles. Cans are rare unless they're huge.

SOEMEK

Something locals do is mix beer and soju. Warning! Please drink slowly!

MAKGEOLLI

A rice wine that I insist you drink chilled. It's thick and sometimes flavored with fruit and has a bit of a bubbly fermented characteristic. Some people love it, some just sample it.

Where to Drink

HOFS

On the windows of pubs in Korea, you'll see the word 'Hof' in English or 호프 in Korean. These drinking holes sell draft beer like Hite or Cass (read: easy to drink/chug). It's common practice to order appetizers with your beers...and depending on who you're drinking with, a bottle of Soju usually finds its way to your table, too. Drink slowly!

POJANG MACHA

I always end up at a Pojang Macha when I'm already a little bit tipsy. This is nothing more than a tent with chairs and an array of fried food like squid and egg rolls! Order a beer or a soju! Keep an eye out for these as you wander Korea!

FRIED CHICKEN SPOTS

Pro Tip: If you want to drink with Koreans, just look for a fried chicken place. Fried chicken and beer are an after-work staple in Korea.

NOREABANGS

Singing rooms or Karaoke rooms are where Koreans will sing and drink until all hours of the night. There are usually waiters who bring beer after beer while you lose track of time in your windowless music box. If someone invites you to a singing room, just know that you'll be drinking until sunrise.

Some Tips on Korean Drinking Culture...

→ Your drink will never be empty while drinking with friends. It is your friend's duty to refill your drink. It can be a slippery slope. When you're ready to stop drinking, just leave your glass half full.

→ Koreans seem to "cheers" every 5 minutes or so! Be prepared to take little sips.

→ Drinking is part of bonding culture and will carry on well into the night - but do not be shy of standing your ground when it's time for you to go home!

→ Pour with two hands as a sign of respect.

Convenience Store Culture 101

In the fast-paced life of Korean students and businessmen, the convenience stores have impressively stepped up to feed the masses. You can find ramen galore and premade meals in any and every convenience store that are actually delicious.

Keep an eye out for this triangle-wrapped kimbap called Samgak-kimbap which comes with many different fillings. BUT make sure to follow the 1-2-3 steps in unwrapping this bad boy or you'll end up with a mess.

While you can often eat inside of convenience stores, drinking beer inside of a convenience store is not usually allowed...but drinking on the curb in front of a convenience store is my jam.

CULTURAL ETIQUETTE

South Korean culture is one of the most unique in the world but also one of the most homogeneous: people do things a certain way and at certain times. While tourists get somewhat of a free pass for not knowing all of the detailed ins and outs, it's good to familiarize yourself with some of the basics to avoid embarrassing missteps.

Tips and Advice

WHAT TO DO...AND NOT TO DO IN SOUTH KOREA

DON'TS

✗ **Don't Pour Your Own Alcohol.** Serving yourself a drink is considered rude, so wait for someone at the table to offer to pour it for you. Trust me, you won't be waiting long!

✗ **Don't Write Anyone's Name Using Red Ink.** Traditionally, red ink was used in funeral rites to write the name of the deceased person. If you write the name of someone still living using a red pen, that actually suggests that you wish they were dead!

✗ **Don't Blow Your Nose in Public.** Koreans find this extremely rude (and honestly, who can blame them?). If you've got the sniffles, excuse yourself and go to the restroom to take care of it.

✗ **Don't Argue if Someone Insists on Paying the Bill.** It's common in South Korea for the oldest person or the person who invited you to pick up the tab at dinner or a bar.

✗ **Don't Talk Loudly on Public Transportation.** Trains and buses are largely silent in South Korea, and you don't want to be that foreigner who disrupts the peace and quiet. Set your phone on silent or vibrate, refrain from making calls, and speak in a low tone if you want to chat with your travel companion.

✗ **Don't Expose Your Shoulders or Cleavage.** South Korean women, especially younger women, will wear short skirts even in the middle of winter, but they rarely wear tops that bare their shoulders or show too much cleavage. To avoid disapproving stares, try to follow these same modesty guidelines!

✗ Don't Be Offended if Someone Asks Your Age. Korean culture runs on an age-based hierarchy, so it's common for people to ask how old you are. That way, they know the proper way to address you.

✗ Don't Touch Strangers. Use your "manner hands" even when taking pictures with strangers. That means, mind where your hands are. Do that awkward hover hand thing.

✗ Don't Place Your Chopsticks Parallel to Each Other Across the Top of a Rice Bowl. This is considered a rude gesture. There will likely be little chopstick holders provided on the table.

✗ Don't Put Unwanted Food in a Used Rice Bowl. Another rude gesture.

✗ Don't Pick up Your Rice Bowl and Bring it Close to Your Mouth. This is also considered rude. Instead, leave your bowl on the table and just bend over it.

✗ Don't Cause Koreans to Lose Face. This is huge in Korea. Saving Face basically means to not embarrass yourself or allow someone else to embarrass you or belittle you. If you insult someone in Korea and cause them to lose face, you're basically asking for a fight because Koreans will not stand for being disrespected.

DO'S

✓ Do Use Two Hands When Shaking Hands, Giving or Receiving Money, or Accepting a Drink. This is considered a sign of respect.

✓ Do Pour Alcohol for Your Companions. Remember, it's rude to pour your own drink. So, help your dining companions out and keep their glasses full! When you pour, use one hand to hold the bottle and touch your other hand to the pouring arm's elbow. You may pour your drink last if no one has poured you a drink yet.

✓ Do Pay Attention to and Respect Priority Seating on Public Transportation. There are designated seats for elderly, disabled, and pregnant passengers. While it's okay for you to sit in these if no one else needs the seat, make sure you pay attention and offer the seat if a priority passenger comes aboard.

✓ **Do Bow.** Bowing is an important part of South Korean etiquette. Bow from the waist and keep your hands folded across your stomach. Different degrees of bow denote different levels of respect and hierarchy, so play it safe and bow just a little bit deeper than the person you're talking to.

✓ **Do Be Ready to Take off Your Shoes.** Many Koreans eat and sit on the floor, so keeping things clean is a must. Wear shoes that are easy to slip on and off so you can remove them in restaurants of people's homes as needed.

✓ **Do Give your Seat to Older People on Public Transportation:** Honestly, this one is fun and respectful. Nothing brings me more joy than the smile of a Korean ajumma when you get up to offer your seat for them.

✓ **Do Wait for Older Companions to Sit Down at Meals First.** This is a sign of respect for your elders. Don't know if someone is older than you? Just wait and let someone else sit down first, and you'll be fine.

South Korea Notes...

....

....

....

....

....

....

Dating Culture

♥ Korea is the land of love! Holidays, restaurant promos, matching outfits, Korean dramas...Koreans love love....and heartbreak. So let me educate you about dating and courtship in SK.

♥ It's common for people to meet potential dates through mutual friends. So, if you pick up some Korean pals, don't be surprised if they offer to introduce you to their single male friends.

♥ Korea is a huge gift-giving culture so it's not uncommon to be given a small bouquet of flowers or a sweet treat on a date.

♥ Men will typically pay for the first few dates, but it's common to split the bill as you get to know each other better.

♥ PDA is acceptable as long as it's not too scandalous! It's perfectly fine for couples to hold hands, hug, or give small kisses in public; just save the make-out sessions for private!

♥ You won't need to worry about a Korean guy ghosting or not answering your texts. Koreans seem to keep in near-constant communication! In fact, it's considered rude if you don't text someone right after a first date to let them know you had a good time.

♥ If you find yourself in a longer-term relationship, get ready for lots of couple's holidays, anniversaries, and matching outfits. Korean couples celebrate Valentine's Day, as well as other relationship holidays like White Day, Pepero Day, and even Christmas as a lovers' holiday. On Valentine's Day, women buy gifts for the men and on White Day, men return the favor and buy gifts for women.

♥ Korean couples celebrate anniversaries in 100-day increments, and it's not uncommon to buy each other rings as a sign of commitment after their first 100 days of dating. You'll also see young Korean couples wearing color-coordinated or even matching clothes.

♥ Bumble, Tinder and OkCupid are common for both foreigners and Koreans to use to find a love match.

♥ Interested in dating another traveler? Just go out on a Friday night to one of the popular bars (like Thursday Party) or go on Bumble and I promise you'll be wifed up in no time.

Important to Note: Korean women don't always approve of their most eligible Korean men dating foreign girls. My friends and I commonly received the cold shoulder or straight up c*ock-blocking from Korean girls protecting their "brothers" (the term commonly used for close friends of similar age). Some Korean girls are fine with it. You'll see.

Fun Fact! South Korean friendships are very touchy-feely, with lots of hand-holding and hugging, even among men.

THE IMPORTANT STUFF: LOGISTICS & ADVICE

How to Budget for South Korea

On the long list of things to love about South Korea, this is a big one - it's crazy affordable to travel. Of course, if you really try, you can make it an expensive trip, but unless you're trying to travel like royalty, it's pretty easy to stay on budget!

BUDGET 💵

Stay in hostels, eat street food, buy snacks and alcohol at convenience stores, travel between cities by bus, and forego big tours. For souvenirs, think market stalls or Daiso (a large dollar store chain with tons of cute and kitschy stuff!).

BALANCED 💵 💵

Stay at lower-tier hotels, eat at mom-and-pop Korean restaurants, ride the high-speed train between cities, pick just one tour to do, but give yourself permission for a few larger splurges along the way, like a night or two at a fancy hotel or tickets to a K-pop concert.

BOUGIE 💵 💵 💵

Free rein! Stay at high-end brand name hotels, do every tour your heart desires, eat at fancy western-style restaurants, fly between cities. Looking for a glitzy souvenir? Splurge on your own hanbok!

	BUDGET	BALANCED	BOUGIE
TOTAL PER DAY	**$70-85**	**$100-140**	**$200+**

All 3 of these options are possible, easy and will offer you the trip of a lifetime – as long as you plan it right.

DAILY EXPENSES

Prices vary depending on where you are on the island, but here's a general estimate of what you'll be spending...

Street Food	$1-8
Traditional Korean Food	$7-12
Convenience Store Food	$2-10
Food at mid-priced restaurant	$10-20
Fancy western-style restaurant	$25-50
Convenience store beer **Convenience store soju**	Around $2.5 Around $1.5
Beer at standard bar	$3-5 ($7-8 for fancy craft beer)
1 Night at a hostel	$14-30
1 Night at a mid-priced hotel	$50-100
1 Night at a ritzy hotel	$150+
Bus ride (within a city)	$1-4
Subway ride (within a city)	$1-6
Taxi ride	$2-10
Train between cities (one way)	$50
Domestic flight (one way)	Most of the time, even on holidays, a domestic flight in Korean cities costs as low as $15-$20 USD!

HOW TO SEE SOUTH KOREA ON A BUDGET

- ◊ Travel during the low season (March-May or September-November).
- ◊ Buy alcohol, snacks, and one meal per day at convenience stores.
- ◊ Sleep in jjimjilbangs
- ◊ Take advantage of free museums and temples!
- ◊ Make a night out of pojangmacha-hopping.
- ◊ Enjoy the natural beauty - hiking and hanging out in the country's many green spaces is free!
- ◊ Head to university areas for cheap souvenir and clothes shopping.
- ◊ Visit cultural centers and tourist information centers for info on free cultural experiences.

YOUR BIGGEST EXPENSES WILL BE:

- ◊ Inter-city travel
- ◊ Lodging
- ◊ Tours

"THE IMPULSE TO TRAVEL IS ONE OF THE HOPEFUL SYMPTOMS OF LIFE"

- Agnes Repplier

Transportation in South Korea

Getting around South Korea might seem intimidating at first. A map of the Seoul subway system scared me so badly that I decided not to apply to teach at any schools in Seoul...but after my first visit and attempt to ride the Seoul subway system, I actually found that it was generally pretty westerner-friendly, at least in the major cities.

Korea is brilliant at everything they do. So, it's not surprising to learn that the public transport systems run extremely smoothly and reliably.

Add in a few handy apps (that I'll introduce you to in a moment) and you'll be traveling like a local in no time.

First, though, let's talk about T-Money. No, that's not a South Korean rapper. It's a rechargeable card that you can use on buses, subways, trains, and even taxis across the country. Load it up and just swipe and go - no messing with individual paper tickets.

When you arrive in Korea, buy a T-Money Card on day 1.

How Much: Buy the basic card for $2.50. Turn it in at the subway station before you leave the country, and you'll be refunded any remaining money that's on the card up to $16.

Where: Buy your card at any subway station booth, bus kiosk, or convenience store showing the T-Money logo.

Bonus! The T-Money card gives you a small discount per trip compared to paper tickets. You can also use it at certain convenience stores and vending machines.

What if you Get Lost? It's going to happen! I occasionally got on the wrong bus or the subway going in the wrong direction - and a local person always helped me out. Don't be afraid to ask for help. You're not in danger. If you do get lost, you'll end up with some great travel stories!

Go here to read the most ridiculous story of the time I got lost and ended up in the back of a police car...

Ways to Move around South Korea

Before I overload you with the fine print, let me tell you my quick thoughts on transport.

1. Taxis are cheap and easy. $10 for a 20-minute ride isn't bad! Especially when you consider that a subway might take 3x the amount of time.

2. I love buses. I usually preferred taking the bus in South Korea over the subway just to get views of the city.

3. The subway system is brilliant, clean and safe. If you come from a city that doesn't have a subway system, it's going to be confusing for you the first couple times...but you'll soon learn that it's so convenient.

4. For inter-city travel, planes are affordable, trains are fast, and buses are cheap.

BY TRAIN

You'll use the train when you're coming to/from the airports or when you're traveling between cities.

Train Company #1

South Korea has an amazing countrywide train system that makes city-to-city travel easy, efficient, and best of all, affordable! A company called

KORAIL operates all passenger trains in the country, and trains generally run from 5am-midnight.

There are a few different major train lines in South Korea:

→Saemul-ho service: This makes the fewest stops and has the cushiest seats. Downside: all seats are reserved.

→Mugunghwa-ho service: This stops at all of the major stops and has both reserved and unreserved seats. Downside: this service tends to be the most popular and thus the most crowded.

→Commute service: This is the cheapest train service. It stops at every stop and only has unreserved seating.

Train Company #2

Then there's the high-speed KTX train service. This has two major lines (the Gyeongbu line and the Honam line) and is the fastest option to get from Point A to Point B. And while it's also the most expensive option, it's definitely not cost-prohibitive. So, this is generally my personal choice!

◊The KORAIL Pass

If your trip includes more than one city, think about purchasing a KORAIL pass. This pass is exclusively for foreigners in South Korea, both tourists and foreign residents. The pass offers unlimited travel on all KORAIL trains, including KTX trains, and is available in 2, 3, 4, or 5 day increments.

There are two types of KORAIL pass:

→**Consecutive:** good for 3 or 5 consecutive days

→**Flexible:** good for 2 or 4 selected days (don't need to be consecutive)

How Much: A KORAIL pass will cost you between $99-172 depending on which package you choose.

Where: You can purchase a pass before you even step foot in South Korea, giving you one less thing to think about when you land all fuzzy and jet-lagged. Go to the KORAIL website at www.letskorail.com; you'll be issued an e-pass, which you'll need to print out to use. You'll use the same website to make seat reservations.

If you don't buy a KORAIL pass ahead of time, you can buy one at the KORAIL office in all the major train stations and airports.

Bonus: KORAIL passes can sometimes get you a discount to certain tourist attractions!

Important Note: The KORAIL pass start date must be within 30 days of purchasing.

BY SUBWAY

Not every South Korean city has a subway system, but the ones that do (Seoul and Busan, for our purposes) do it very well. Getting around by subway (aka metro) is cheap and convenient.

In addition, the signs and station names are almost always given in English as well as Korean, so the subway system is also incredibly foreigner-friendly! Don't see any English signs? Ask a stranger. But to avoid language confusion…

Don't say: *"Excuse me, can you tell me where is the subway to Hongdae?"*
Do Say: *"Hongdae?"*

Keep it simple. And remember to use Naver Maps to find your subway route.

Pro Tip! Avoid traveling on the subway during rush hour. Like in any other big city, public transportation in Seoul and Busan gets packed with commuters!

The best way to utilize the subway system is to purchase a T-money card. This is a rechargeable plastic card.

Where: You buy your ticket or load up your T-Money card at the automated kiosks located at the entrance of every station.

How Much: It'll vary depending on where you're going, obviously, but the basic fare (up to 6 miles) costs about $1.25.

Last Tip for Subways: Use the lockers located in Subway stops if you want to store your gear while you go out to party or explore! The lockers are extremely safe. You can feel comfortable leaving your valuables here! Just make sure you remember which subway station you left your things in!

BY BUS

If the subway system still intimidates you, then you will find peace by using the bus system (plus, you get views of the city!).

South Korea has an extensive, reliable, and clean bus system. You'll definitely find yourself hopping on a bus if you venture outside Seoul and Busan, or even within those two cities to reach some more out-of-the-way sights.

Buses often don't run at specific times, but they come around every 10-15 minutes, and many bus stops have an electronic sign telling you when the next bus will be there. You'll board the bus in the front and pay your fare there (with your T-Money card).

Download the KakaoBus app and find a bus route near you + get a view of the city as you ride. Use NaverMaps while you're on the bus to track when you're approaching your destination.

Pro Tip! Most people get tripped up when it comes to knowing when to get off the local buses. Some buses will announce (either on speaker or on a digital sign near the driver) the name of the approaching stop. Depending where you are, it might be written in English, it might not. It's helpful to ask someone on the bus if you're getting off at the right stop (or just show them the name of where you want to go on your phone). Koreans are helpful.

There are three types of buses in South Korea:

1. Local Bus (getting around the city)

Traveling within a city is easy on the bus! You will see bus stops everywhere you walk! Use KakaoBus to find the correct bus stop near you.

How Much: Anywhere from $.90 to $2 depending on where you're riding to.

Where: South Korean bus stops are pretty standard looking, so you'll see them along the sidewalk! Pay in cash or use your T-Money card when you board the bus.

Not Important Unless You're Living Here Long-Term: Most cities have two local bus lines. The Jwaseok line is more expensive, but you're guaranteed a seat and people aren't allowed to stand. The Ilban line is cheaper but has fewer seats and standing is allowed. Both lines run pretty much the same routes and run with the same frequency.

2. Regional Bus

You can use these buses to get from city to city within South Korea. There are two main regional lines. The Gosok buses are high-speed, operate over the longest distances, and make very few stops. The Shioe buses are slower, go shorter distances, and make more stops.

How Much: Plan for $18-25.

Where: These buses tend to leave from each city's major bus terminal (typically located near a major train/subway station). Buy your ticket at the bus station.

3. Incheon Airport Bus Service

These are buses that go from Incheon Airport to several major cities in South Korea.

How Much: $7-15

Where: When arriving at Incheon Airport, you can get a bus to practically whichever big city you want to go to! Buy your ticket at the offices located inside Exit 4 and 9 in Arrival Hall Floor 1 or outside Exits 4, 6, 7, 8, 11, 13, and 9C. Your ticket will tell you which stop to go to.

To take the Incheon Airport Bus from your city to the airport, have your hotel help you arrange it!

To learn how to book a bus ticket like a pro, I recommend checking out this awesome girl's step-by-step blog:

BY TAXI

Compared to a lot of other countries, taxi rides in South Korea are actually really reasonably priced. You can grab a taxi from the taxi stands at most train and bus stations and tourist attractions, or you can hail a taxi off the street by raising your arm palm down.

There are two types of taxis in most South Korean cities:

Regular: These are cheaper and more common. Fares start at $2.75 for the first 1.25 miles, and there is a 20 percent surcharge from midnight to 4am.

Warning: regular taxis will occasionally pick up additional passengers who are going the same direction as you. This action, Hapseung, is technically illegal but some drivers still do it, especially during rush hour.

Deluxe: These taxis are fancier and more expensive. They are black with yellow tops. They charge $4.50 for the first 1.8 miles but they don't charge a late-night fee.

Almost all taxis will be metered; if you come across one that isn't, negotiate the fare before starting your ride! Tipping is not required. It's also a good idea to have your translation app pulled up or to have the name and address of where you want to go in hangul to better communicate with your driver.

BY CAR

You can definitely count on using public transportation and taxis exclusively in the big cities. But if your trip includes time in a more out-of-the-way place, like Jeju Island, you might want to consider renting a car.

Driving can be kind of a trip in South Korea, though, so be prepared. They drive fast and aggressively, particularly buses and trucks.

You'll need to get an international driver's license before you get to South Korea. You can do this at your local AAA for about $20.

UBER

...exists only in Seoul, at the moment. Uber Black is the most common car to find and it's expensive!

Internet in South Korea

Oh, Korean Wi-Fi . . . I could write a sonnet about it because it's just that good. As of 2017, South Korea had the fastest average internet connection in the world, and you can connect to free public Wi-Fi virtually everywhere.

Where to Get Internet:

At the airport when you land, you can get unlimited data plans immediately! The SIM card plans are sold, usually, by how many days you'll be in the country (5-60) making it easy to choose your plan.

Forgot to pick up a SIM at the airport? Most convenience stores will sell you a SIM card and if you signal to the cashier that you are foreign and helpless, they will even help you set it up on the spot.

30 days will cost you about $60 USD or $2 per day - which is a great deal for a no-contract phone plan!

Pro Tip! Make sure your phone is unlocked before you travel!

If you can't unlock your phone or you want to make extra sure you're always connected, you can also pick up a pocket wi-fi device ("wi-fi egg") from...

→ Pocket Wi-Fi Korea (www.pocketwifikorea.com)

→ Package Korea (www.packagekorea.com)

→ or Link Korea (www.linkkorea.co.kr)

These will run you around $5 per day and you can pick them up at the airport.

NAVER MAP

Forget Google Maps. Korea runs on Naver Map, a much more detailed and reliable map system for this region. It gives you a good visual orientation on Seoul's sometimes winding streets. You can also save and download locations so you can show them to a taxi driver or local if you get lost.

NAVER DICTIONARY AND TRANSLATE

This is a lifesaver if you need to ask a detailed question, like asking for directions. Many South Koreans are happy to write back and forth to answer your questions.

VISIT KOREA

Made by the Korea Tourism Board, you can download this app right now to help you plan your trip around festivals and events.

KAKAOTALK OR WHATSAPP

These are the most common messaging apps in South Korea and allow you to both text and call.

SUBWAY KOREA

This app gives you train and bus routes, as well as updated timetables. It even tells you which train car to board for the quickest exit and transfer!

KAKAOMETRO

Staying in Seoul? This is another app to download if you're planning on taking the metro/subway.

KAKAO TAXI

Can't find a cab after a night out in Gangnam? No need to worry with Kakao Taxi! Just hail a ride through the app and a cab will be headed straight to you in minutes.

XE

This is a currency converter that will help you quickly convert prices to avoid getting ripped off or spending beyond your means!

MANGOPLATE

Like Yelp or TripAdvisor for food and restaurants in Korea! On this app, you'll find many restaurants that are not located elsewhere.

YOGIYO

Korea's most popular food-ordering app, which is basically like UberEats.

SAFETY 101

Activities to Avoid in South Korea

1. Eating Shark Fin.

Shark fin is a status symbol in South Korea and can be found in soup, dumplings, and other menu items. It's a cruel delicacy: finned sharks are often thrown back into the ocean still alive, leaving them to starve or bleed to death or be eaten by predators. Overfishing has also caused at least one-third of oceanic shark species to become endangered. Choose more sustainable and less cruel seafood options.

2. Going to "Buy Me Drinky" Bars.

These are "hostess" bars where patrons (usually creepy men) pay to drink with attractive (sometimes scantily clad) women, both Korean and foreign. They're common hangouts for Korean businessmen, foreign male travelers and military service members. While these bars are not dangerous, they are absolutely sleazy and one can also assume...offer illicit services.

3. Eating Dog Meat.

Dog meat is a traditional Korean delicacy, eaten most often in the heat of the summer by older Korean men. The industry is incredibly cruel, and there's been large international outrage in recent years over Korea's dog meat markets. Traditional belief has it that dog meat increases men's virility, and that creating a surge of adrenaline through the animal in the last moments of its life (essentially done through torture) enhances these effects. Don't support this industry! This is one case where you can refuse food that is offered to you and express your opposition.

Scams to Watch Out for

1. Fake Monks.

If you see a Buddhist priest or monk on the street soliciting donations, don't be fooled - that is NOT a real monk. Fake monks hassling tourists for money have become a well-known scam in South Korea in recent years. If you encounter one of these scam artists, just politely walk away.

2. Pickpockets.

Crime is pretty rare in South Korea but you do have to keep an eye out for theft in crowded areas. Pickpockets often work in pairs or groups; one person distracts you by bumping into you or striking up a conversation while another person slits the bottom of your purse and makes off with your stuff. When you're in a crowd, stay aware of your belongings and keep your purse in front of your body.

3. Phone Theft.

On a recent season of 90 Day Fiancé, one of the Korean love interests confessed that his last job was reselling stolen phones. These phones are often swiped at the bars. Keep your phone in your purse and your purse zipped. A purse is much less likely to be stolen than a phone.

4. Fake Prices for Tourists.

Some shady restaurants, shops, or vendor stalls will try to bill tourists by charging more than the stated price for goods and services. Don't be afraid to point out the listed price if you feel like you're getting overcharged.

5. Fake Ceremonies.

In recent years, there have been more reports about a scam involving a fake Korean ceremony. Foreigners will be approached by a woman or a couple of women and asked if they've recently had a loved one pass away. If you say yes, the women will then tell you that your loved one's soul is not at peace and that they can help by performing a traditional spiritual ceremony - for a fee, of course. This is not a real thing, so don't fall for it.

Safe Girl Tips for South Korea

One of my most favorite things about South Korea — and there are a LOT! — is how safe it is. Violent crime is virtually non-existent, especially for tourists, and even petty theft is rare. Generally speaking, single gal travelers can feel safe and secure to just relax and enjoy their trip! Here are just a few common sense things to know about safety in South Korea.

◊ Be Wary on the Roads

Drivers in South Korea like to go fast — and by fast, I mean FAST! Buses in particular can occasionally seem like they're reenacting a scene from Speed. Always wear your seat belt when you're in a taxi or other vehicle, and be extremely careful when crossing roads, even with a walk signal. Same goes for when you cross alleys or driveways. Look both ways and then look again.

◊ Trust Your Gut

It's easy and fun to get off the beaten track in South Korea, and I highly encourage you to do so! But you should still listen to your intuition. Don't go wandering down dark, deserted alleys by yourself at night.

◊ Watch Your Drinks

Drink-spiking isn't a huge trend in South Korea, but it still happens occasionally. Just like at home, don't leave your drink unattended.

◊ Know your Alcohol Limits

You will never be able to keep up with a Korean who has been marathon drinking since the age of 19, I guarantee it. And be aware of your limits. South Koreans like to drink. In fact, drinking culture is part of work culture. It's easy to feel pressured to keep up. Don't be afraid to call it a night!

◊ Keep an Eye on Your Purse and Phone

Yes, I said petty theft is rare, but pickpockets do still exist in South Korea.

When you're in crowded, touristy areas, keep your purse in front of your body so you can keep an eye on it.

...MASSIVE EXCEPTION: IF A KOREAN WOMAN GRABS YOUR PURSE ON THE BUS OR TRAIN

One of my favorite delights of Korean culture is this! Let's say you get on a bus and it's packed. Grandma has a comfortable seat, but you are carrying a big purse, backpack or groceries. Grandma might, without saying a word, grab your haul out of your hands and place it on her lap until it's your stop to get off. ISN'T THAT THE LOVELIEST THING EVER?!

◊ *Watch out for Ticks*

If you're planning to hike in South Korea, be on the look-out for ticks, which carry some not-so-fun diseases. Wear long sleeves and pants and/or stock up on some strong bug spray.

◊ *Sexual Assault*

You are more likely to be sexually assaulted by a foreign man (i.e., a fellow tourist) than you are to be assaulted by a South Korean man. Keep your wits about you, particularly when staying in hostels. Watch how much you're drinking, be aware of your surroundings, and again, trust your gut.

◊ *Avoid Political Protests*

From time to time, you'll see South Koreans protesting everything from relations with the North to the presence of American military personnel. Just keep walking. It's actually illegal for foreigners to join in on protests in South Korea, so you don't want to accidentally look like you're a part of it.

A Word about North Korea...

For a lot of people, the first thing that jumps to mind when they think about South Korea is North Korea. Obviously, the political situation on the peninsula remains somewhat tense despite the climactic peace treaty reached between North and South in 2017, so just do your research before planning your trip. Check out the U.S. State Department travel advisories and keep an eye on the news so you have an idea of where relations stand.

Alexa's Pro Tips
FOR SOUTH KOREA

You've already learned basic South Korean etiquette, but here are a few more tips I wish someone had told me when I arrived in Korea on day one!

◊ *Make Friends with a Korean*

I'm not going to lie. Korea can be a discombobulating country to be suddenly dropped into! It is incredibly helpful to have a local friend. So ask your friends if they know anyone willing to meet you in South Korea, go on a dating app and find a local (of use Bumble BFF), sign up for a tour on GetYourGuide or just make it a priority to talk to strangers.

◊ *Don't Be Surprised or Offended if you get blatantly stared at...*

...especially by older people. For the most part, they don't mean to be rude—they're just curious. Remember, South Korea is still a very homogenous culture and you, an intrepid traveler, stand out! That being said, if you find yourself getting stared at, a lot, by multiple people, just do a quick check-in to make sure you're not accidentally doing something rude (talking on your phone or listening to loud music on public transport, showing a lot of cleavage, etc.).

◊ *Carry Tissues*

You'll occasionally come across a Korean bathroom that does not have toilet paper, so it's good to have a stash of tissues in your purse.

◊ *Carry Cash*

Most stores and restaurants in South Korea do accept credit cards, but it's always a good idea to have some cash on hand, especially if you want to do some street shopping or village wandering.

◊ You Won't Be Able to Try Things on While Shopping

If you're shopping along a shopping street, you can try things on. So, hold whatever you want from shoulder to shoulder as a general rule of thumb to see if something fits. You can try shoes on and you can try things on in department stores.

◊ Take Advantage of Free Travel Services

If your hotel has a concierge, use it! Nine times out of ten, you can trust their recommendations (they're not just s ending you to their friends' places), and having some ideas of where to start can help narrow down South Korea's sometimes overwhelming list of things to do. Also keep an eye out for tourist information centers; they generally have English-speaking staff or resources, plus free wi-fi, phone chargers, and air conditioning/heat!

◊ Wear Comfortable Shoes that are easy to take on and off.

More traditional Korean restaurants will ask you to remove your shoes and you don't want to have to fuss with a lot of laces or buckles. Also, you'll be walking a LOT (and going up and down a ton of stairs in the subway system!) so you want to be comfortable.

◊ Be Prepared for a Lack of English

Despite its status as a business and tourist destination, South Korea still has a surprising lack of English signage (besides in transportation hubs). In addition, many people speak only a word or two of English, even young people in urban areas. Be ready with your translation app, learn a few basic Korean phrases, and brush up on your charade skills. Most importantly, be patient. The majority of people do want to help you and are trying!

◊ Let Go of Your Idea of Personal Space

Personal space just doesn't exist here. You will get bumped into, pushed up against, and generally have your personal bubble popped. Just like the staring, nine times out of ten, people don't mean anything by it, so stay calm and go with the flow!

◊ Squatter Toilets

I'd be totally remiss if I didn't warn you about the squatter toilets. While most places will have western-style toilets, unless you're going way out into the countryside, you still might run into a scenario where you find yourself having to use one of these. There are sometimes signs showing you the right and wrong way to use a squatter toilet, but basically you want to squat over the hole facing the wall of the toilet (where the flusher is), not facing forward like you would on a regular western-style toilet. To flush, you may need to use a bucket of water. In that case, hold the bucket up high when you pour the water in the hole, to create a pressure system.

To learn how to pee in a hole in the ground, I've made you a quick tutorial video.

◊ Fixed Doors

A lot of establishments in South Korea have double entrance doors but one side will be perpetually locked. A fire hazard? Maybe, but that's just the way it is. Most of the time there will be a sign in English saying "fixed."

◊ Glass Doors Have a Button to Open Them

I still remember the day where I stood in front of a cafe trying to enter like an idiot while the entire staff looked at me like a weirdo.

REMEMBER. ANYONE WHO DOESN'T SUPPORT YOU TAKING THIS TRIP DOUBTS THEIR OWN ABILITY TO TRAVEL...NOT YOURS.

KOREAN LANGUAGE 101

Despite how futuristic and international Koreans are, English is not that widely spoken in South Korea. So, you will be a) relying on translating apps often and b) will really benefit from learning how to speak and read just a little bit of the Korean language!

LEARN TO READ KOREAN

Traveling around South Korea is infinitely easier when you can read signs, menus, etc. But don't worry, I'm not going to load you up with textbooks and tell you to study for hours! The truth is, it's actually super easy to learn to read and write the Korean language - you can do it in a day!

Before we jump right into it, here are a few things you should know about the Korean written language.

Koreans read and write using an alphabet called hangul. It was invented in the 1400s and is hugely important to Korean culture. Before hangul was invented, Koreans wrote using classical Chinese characters, which are super complicated and required lots of education. This meant that most people couldn't read or write at all. The introduction of hangul opened up written language to Koreans of all classes because it was much more efficient and easier to learn and use.

Koreans are immensely proud of hangul, and there's even a national holiday in October celebrating the birth of the language!

Okay, enough history. Let's get down to business. To learn to read and write hangul, you need to master a whopping 24 letters - 14 consonants and 10 vowels. Yup, that's it. Once you learn those characters, you'll be able to sound out just about any word you see written in Korean.

There are a ton of resources out there online to help you learn hangul, but here are a couple of my favorites:

Learn to Read Korean
in 15 Minutes

Great easy visual reminders to
work on your syllables!

Even if you spend just an hour on the plane, you can pick up the hangul basics and make your trip so much easier and more enjoyable. Bonus - you'll wow other tourists when you just breezily translate a menu for them!

ESSENTIAL KOREAN PHRASES

First, I cannot stress this enough. You won't actually start impeccably speaking or hearing Korean until you're in an atmosphere where it's being used all the time. This language takes practice both for your ears to hear it and for your mouth to speak it.

Get a head start in this section but be gentle with yourself. The language will come to you after a couple days in Korea!

Pro Tip! Use the app called Duolingo to learn and practice Korean!

GREETINGS	
Hi	Annyeong *(informal, casual)*
Hello	Annyeong-haseyo *(most commonly used and slightly more formal)*
Hello	Annyeong-hashim-nika *(most formal)*
Goodbye	Annyeong *(informal and casual - use this with friends. And yes, it's the same as hello!)*
Goodbye if the other person is leaving	Jal-ga-yo *OR* an-nyeong-hi-ga-se-yo

Goodbye if you are leaving	N-nyeong-hi-gye-se-yo
Have a safe journey	Jo-shim-hi-ga-se-yo
Bye	*Bai (just like in English)*

And if you panic and forget everything...say *Ba-i*.

USEFUL PHRASES	
Thank You	Gam-sa-ham-nida
No, thank you/ you're welcome:	Gwen-chanayo
Please	Juseyo *(For example, to say, "Water, please" you'd say "Mul, juseyo)*
Excuse me (when passing someone)	Jamsi-manyo
I'm sorry	Jeo-song-abnida
Goodbye if you are leaving	N-nyeong-hi-gye-se-yo
Have a safe journey	Jo-shim-hi-ga-se-yo
Yes	Ne
No	Aniyo
My name is	Jeh-ellumen ____ ibnida
What is your name?	I-reumi mwo-yeyo?
It's nice to meet you	Manna-seo banga-awayo
I don't understand	I-hae-ga an doe-yo
Where is the restroom?	Hwa-zang-sil eodie so yo?

Quick Lesson: "*Hwa-zang-sil*" means restroom and "*eodie?*" is how to ask where something is.

AT THE RESTAURANT	
Excuse Me (To Get Someone's Attention, Like In A Restaurant)	Jo-giyo
Please Bring The Check	Gyesan-hae juseyo
It's Okay	Gwen chang ah
How Much Does It Cost?	Erl ma ye yo
How Much Is This?	Jaw gaw erl ma ye yo?
Delicious	Mashita
Cheers	Geon-bae
Water	Mul
Beer	Mekju
Tea	Cha
Meat	Go-gee
Pork	Dwaeji gogee
Beef	Soe gogee
Chicken	Dak
Fried Chicken	You'll often just hear *"chikin"*
Fish	Mul gogi *(literal translation is "water meat")*
Shrimp	Saeu
Rice	Bap
Dessert	Dijeo-teu
Vegetarian	Chae-sig-ju-uija
I'm A Vegetarian	Jeo-neun chae-sig-haeyo
Spicy	Mae-un
Not Spicy	Maebji anh-eun

To Ask for Not Spicy	Maeun-geo ppae-juseyo *(Literally means "please take out anything spicy")*
A Little Spicy	Yaggan maeun

MUST-KNOW	
Left	Oen-joe
Right	Oleun-joej
Straight	Jik-jin
Older Man	Ajushi
Older Woman	Ajumma
Foreigner (slang)	Wayguk
Foreigner (proper)	Way-gukin
Fire!	Bul iya
Call the Police	Gyeongchal-eul bule-uda
Help!	Wowajuseyo
Stop!	Meom-chuda
Stop! (slang)	Hajima! (this is the one I usually use with my students)

Quick Lesson: Adding "jima" to the end of some words makes them negative. For example, "mok" means eat. "Mokjima" means "don't eat!". So, if you're hearing "jima" at the end of a word, take a second to pause what you're doing.

Don't know the word in English? Here's a hack that will work 25% of the time...

Add "uh" to English words and Koreans just might understand you. An easy example: McDonalds becomes "Mac-uh-don-ulds-uh". In the Korean language syllables are divided carefully not only in speaking but in writing. Each block of characters stands for one syllable. This makes sense.

Phew. You have just consumed two years of Korean culture in just a few pages. You are officially more prepared than the average traveler!

Now, you're ready to get on a plane! So, what do you do when you arrive in Korea? It depends where you're flying into. The three major airports are in Seoul, Incheon and Busan. In each of these chapters, I'll give you an airport run down that will help you navigate your first few hours on the ground.

Okay, you're earned it...let's get to the fun stuff!

Nervous?

Even I get nervous before (and during) a new trip. The secret? Turn that nervous energy into excited energy. Instead of saying *"I'm afraid to do this"* say *"I can't wait to do this"* and let life happen.

CHAPTER ONE

—

Seoul

—

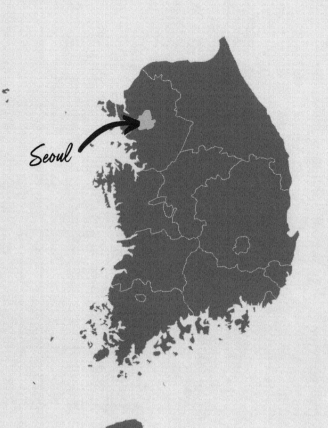

Seoul

INTRODUCTION TO SEOUL

The most traditional yet most futuristic city on this planet is Seoul.

One moment you could be roaming an ancient world heritage site and the next, partying your face off Gangnam Style under the bright city lights.

South Korea's capital city of just under 10 million people blends ancient culture and modern technology in a surprising yet seamless way.

South Koreans are fiercely proud of their "Miracle on the Han," (referring to this city built on the Han River) and as they should be. The city skyrocketed to economic success after the Korean War and has become a major international business and tourism destination for the world's most powerful people and industries.

That being said, Seoul is huge. The city is divided by a river, connected by an extremely intricate subway system and can take you over an hour to get from one side of the city to the next. So, make sure you choose where you stay based on what you plan to do in the city!

As you're about to see, your Seoul experience can be completely customized to your heart's desire (especially if your heart desires food).

You can go on a peaceful early morning temple or palace tour, followed by a graceful tea ceremony in Bukchon Hanok Village. Snack on kimchi nachos and other fusion dreams with the expat crowd in Itaewon. Hit the Rodeo Drive of Seoul in Apgujeong and the city's foodie paradise in Hapjeong. Dance and drink the night away in Hongdae. Whatever reality you wish, you can create. So, let's do that now by introducing you to the most relevant neighborhoods in Seoul!

From the Airport in Seoul

There are two airports in Seoul: Incheon Airport and Gimpo Airport.

✈ **Incheon Airport** is South Korea's main international airport, located about 30 miles outside of the city itself.

✈ **Gimpo Airport** is used as Korea's main domestic airport, with flights to Busan, Jeju, etc.

Need to transfer between Incheon Airport and Gimpo Airport?

Easy. You have two options.

→ **Option #1:** Take the Airport Express (AREX) All Stop Train which is located inside of both airports. Traveling between Incheon and Gimpo takes about 35 minutes with 5 stops in between and costs around 3,550 won.

→ **Option #2:** Take the bus from Incheon, located in Terminal 1, to Gimpo. The bus leaves every 20 minutes, takes about 46 minutes and the journey costs less than 9 KRW. The other direction, from Gimpo to Incheon, takes about 40 minutes and costs 7,500 KRW.

Now, how do you get from the airport to your hotel?

FROM INCHEON AIRPORT

→ **Option 1: Airport Train**

Hopping on the AREX Airport Railroad is your best bet. You can take the Express train, which goes non-stop to Seoul Station, or the "all stops" commuter train, which stops at nine major stations between the airport and the city (this is the one that stops by Gimpo).

⊙ **How Long:** 45 minutes for the Express train, about an hour for the commuter train

💰 **How Much:** $6.80 for the Express train, $3.60 for the commuter train. You'll also need to put down a deposit for the AREX ticket card; this will cost about 50 cents and you can return your card at the deposit machines near the station exit at your destination.

◉ **When:** Express trains run every 25-40 minutes, while commuter trains run every 10 minutes; trains run between 5:30am and 10:45pm.

♥ **Where:** Buy your ticket at the automated ticketing machines in Terminals 1 and 2 outside of the arrivals gate. You can also find information counters in Terminals 1 and 2, as well as at Incheon's Travel Center in the arrivals area, which will save you some time and point you in the right direction.

Pro Tip: If you fly in with Korean Air, Asiana Airlines, or Jeju Air, you can get a discounted ticket price; go to the information counters to use this discount.

··

→ Option 2: KAL Airport Limousine Bus

Take a comfy seat on the airport bus which will drive you to multiple stations and landmarks throughout the city. A couple of the buses (N6000 to Gangnam and N6001 to Seoul Station) run through the night as well, making this a good option if you land late when the trains aren't running.

◉ **How Long:** 60-70 minutes

💰**How Much:** $11 for a one-way ticket, $21 for roundtrip

◉ **When:** Buses leave around every 30 minutes between 5am and 11pm.

♥ **Where:** Buy your tickets from the machines or booths outside of the arrivals gate, or book in advance online in this code. ☞

··

→ Option 3: Taxi

This is your most expensive option but it's useful if you get in late at night, have a lot of luggage, or just don't feel like waiting around for a bus or train. Try to take a regular taxi instead of a deluxe or jumbo taxi, which seat more people and cost more. Be aware that between midnight and 4am, you'll encounter a night surcharge of 20%.

◉ **How Long:** 60-70 minutes

💰**How Much:** $50-$100 depending on what type of taxi you take and where you're going.

⊙ **When:** Anytime you want! You can find a taxi 24 hours a day.

♀ **Where:** Just follow the signs outside the arrivals gate to find a fleet of taxis.

Pro Tip: If you can, have your destination address or hotel name pulled up on your phone in hangul to make it easier for the driver to know where you're going.

→ **Option 4: Uber**

When you arrive in Seoul, buy a SIM card, connect it to your Uber account (you'll get a verification code) and now you can take the most convenient transportation option alive.

💸 **How Much:** Similar prices to a standard taxi

♀ **Where:** Follow the signs to the designated Uber areas after baggage claim. You're going to Exit 4 for Terminal 1 and Exit 1 for Terminal 2

Pro Tip! You can arrange your Uber airport pick-up up to 30 days in advance! Go here ☞

→ **Option 5: International Taxi**

This is a Taxi service that speaks English, which you need to book ahead of time. I, personally, think it's a big hassle - but if you want to try, here's what you need to know.

☆ **Book:** 24 hours in advance here - www.intltaxi.co.kr/reservation/book

💸 **How Much:** The same price as a standard taxi.

♀ **Where:** After baggage claim, there will be an international taxi stand where you can show them your confirmation and they'll point you in the right direction.

FROM GIMPO AIRPORT

→ *Option 1:* Airport Train

Gimpo also has access to the AREX Airport Railroad. Just like Incheon, you can hop on the All-Stop train which makes multiple stops between the airport and Seoul Station.

◷ *How Long:* 22 minutes.

How Much: Just over $1 USD one-way. You can also put down a deposit for the AREX ticket card; this will cost about 50 cents and you can return your card at the deposit machines near the station exit at your destination.

◷ *When:* Trains run between 5:30am and 10:45pm.

♥ *Where:* After baggage claim, go down the escalators to access the underground station. Head to subway line 5 or 9 to catch the train.

....

→ *Option 2:* Taxi

For the cheapest ride, take the standard orange taxi.

How Much: How much you'll spend depends on where in Seoul you're going, but don't worry, these taxis are affordable (around $20) and the center of Seoul is only 25 minutes away from the airport.

◷ *When:* The standard orange taxis are available 24/7.

♥ *Where:* Head into the arrivals hall and you'll see a sign pointing you in the direction of the taxis.

Pro Tip: You can order an international taxi at Gimpo, just like you can at Incheon. The website spells Gimpo as "Kim-Po".

....

→ *Option 3:* Uber

If you've got a SIM card already, this is my preferred method of transport from the airport.

♥ *Where:* Like many airports, there is a designated waiting area for Uber.

Follow the signs after baggage claim that will direct you to the right spot or ask your drive which gate to meet at!

🏷️**How Much:** Similar prices to a standard taxi

···

→ **Option 4: The 6021 Bus**

Also called the "airport limousine" will take you to many stops, including Seoul Station where you can then get on the subway and carry on to your destination.

⊙ **How Long:** 45 minutes to the center of Seoul

🏷️**How Much:** A one-way ticket costs $6 (7,000 won)

⊙ **When:** 6am to 11:10 pm

♀ **Where:** Catch the 6021 bus outside of the main terminal, to the right of Gate 6 - look for stops 2 and 6.

Now, what do you do when you get to Seoul station? Let's talk about how to get around Seoul...

Getting around Seoul

Public transportation in Seoul is reliable and relatively easy to figure out, despite how overwhelming the maps may look. You'll rely mostly on using the subway and your feet, with a few taxis thrown in here and there. For the most part, you don't need to bother with buses in Seoul.

The first thing you'll want to do is grab a rechargeable fare card like T-money or Seoul City Pass Plus; you can pick these up at convenience stores or at automated machines in most major subway stations. The cards will cost about $2 and you can top up at any station.

Pro Tip: Save this website on your phone to calculate any and all transport routes in Seoul

Subway System

Super foreigner-friendly! Metro signs and announcements are given in both Korean and English, and your pre-paid card makes it a cinch to hop on and off as you please. The evening rush hour (around 4pm-8pm) gets insanely crowded, so you might want to avoid riding during this time. If you do ride during this time, prepare for "the crush" aka when you are squeezed like sardines into one car.

How Much: You can travel up to 6 miles for about $1.50

Pro Tip: Save this website on your phone which will help you calculate your subway routes quickly!

....

Uber

Uber is on a trial period in Seoul but you can use it. Take advantage!

....

Taxi

Taxis in Seoul are pretty affordable, at least compared to other large cities. They're a good option if you're in a hurry or going a short distance. Regular taxis are silver, orange, blue, or white and have a "taxi" sign on their roof. Deluxe taxis are black with a yellow stripe.

Available taxis will have a red light on their roof or inside the windshield on the passenger side. You can find taxi stands at major train and bus stations, tourist attractions, and big hotels. You can also flag a taxi down Carrie Bradshaw-style. Just extend your arm with your hand palm down and motion toward yourself.

How Much: About $2.30 for the first couple of miles in a regular taxi (there's a 20% surcharge from midnight-4am). Deluxe taxis will cost about $3 for the first couple miles, but they don't charge a night fee and you can pay with credit card.

Pro Tip: Tipping isn't common in Korea, but it's good form to just round up your fare and let the driver keep the change.

Bus

Seoul's bus system is also very extensive but it can be a bit more confusing to navigate. Bus maps and announcements are typically only in Korean, and buses are colored differently depending on where they go.

Blue buses are the main line and run throughout most of the city, while yellow buses operate only downtown and green buses run mostly between major stations. Red buses will take you to areas outside of the city itself.

How Much: About $1.50 for a one-way trip.

....

Walking

You'll definitely get your steps in while you're in Seoul! While you won't be able to rely exclusively on walking, going on foot will give you the chance to explore more off-the-beaten-path areas and notice sights you might miss if you're on the train.

Pro Tip: Be VERY careful when crossing streets, as many South Korean drivers do not give pedestrians the right of way.

Fun Fact!

On Valentine's Day, women give their men gifts; on White Day in March, men return the favor; on the world's saddest holiday in April (Black Day), single South Koreans mourn their singleness by eating sticky black noodles.

NEIGHBORHOODS TO KNOW IN SEOUL

HONGDAE

Named for Hongik University, this neighborhood is known for underground art, indie music, and a 24-hour party scene. Find the latest Korean fashions on Hongdae Walking Street and show off your singing skills at one of the neighborhood's quirky noreabangs (private karaoke rooms). Hongdae is a great place to catch K-pop street performances, fill up on street food, and take in Seoul's neon nightlife!

When my friends visit Seoul, I tell them to either stay here or Itaewon (below) as both areas are very walkable. They are western enough to help you navigate but still hold enough Korean charm and culture to delight you.

➤ **Getting There:** Hop on Subway Line 2, get off at Hongik University Station, and go through Exit 9. Follow the crowd and/or your eyes, ears, and nose from there to find all the action!

ITAEWON

The most international neighborhood in all of Seoul used to actually be the most dangerous and dirty (adjectives that are not used to describe many places in Korea these days). But now, Itaewon is the thriving hotspot among expats, foreign travelers, as well as service members from the nearby U.S. military base. Itaewon is also popular with cool, young Koreans.

The shops, restaurants, and clubs in Itaewon are all extremely foreigner-friendly, so it's a great place to meet a diverse group of new friends! You can find everything from upscale western local and international DJs (some of which are pretty famous). I also like Itaewon for its proximity to some of the best temples and museums! It's a great jumping off point to explore the city.

☞ **Getting There:** Take Line 6 of the Seoul Subway and get off at Itaewon Station 6.

GANGNAM

Of course, you can't miss Seoul's most famous neighborhood! This is the Hollywood of South Korea. Think gleaming skyscrapers, glittering city views, and swanky nightclubs with big-name DJs. During the day, this is where you come to shop and sip on (expensive) lattes. During the night, this is where you come to party like a fancy girl.

☞ **Getting There:** Take Seoul Subway Line 2 to Gangnam Station and take Exit 10 or 11 OR take Line 9 to Sinnonhyeon Station and use Exit 5 or 6.

APGUJEONG

The Rodeo Drive of Seoul is not too far from Gangnam. Apgujeong is packed with the biggest names in high-end shopping, think Gucci, Prada, and Armani. The neighborhood is home to dozens of beauty salons and cosmetics stores, as well as some of Korea's world-famous cosmetic surgery clinics. You can also tour iconic filming locations from the country's most popular daytime dramas.

☞ **Getting There:** Get on the Bundang Subway line to Apgujeong Rodeo Station. Take exit 6 and go straight out of the exit, then turn left onto Apgujeong-ro 50-gil.

BUKCHON HANOK VILLAGE

Nestled among some of Seoul's most beautiful palaces and shrines, this historic village will transport you back in time and capture your heart. Bukchon is a residential neighborhood filled with guesthouses, restaurants, tea houses, and cultural centers. Come here to immerse yourself in traditional Korean culture!

Getting There: Take the Seoul Subway Line 3 and get off at Anguk Station; then take Exit 3 and turn right out of the exit.

Pro Tip: Much of Bukchon is closed on Sundays, and some of the cultural experiences require reservations; visit dobo.visitseoul.net for more information.

INSA-DONG

Stroll down Insa-dong's alley-lined main street and take in a dizzying array of art galleries, traditional teahouses, souvenir shops, and cafes. You can watch street performances, sample unique Korean candies, and even have your fortune told. The main street is closed to vehicles on Saturdays and Sundays, turning Insa-dong into a foot-explorer's paradise!

☞ **Getting There:** Take Seoul Subway Line 3 and get off at Anguk Station Exit 6 OR take Seoul Subway Line 1 to Jonggak Station and take Exit 11.

MYEONG-DONG

If you're short on time in Seoul, swing by Myeong-dong where you can get a small, densely-packed bite of everything that Seoul has to offer. You can stock up on skincare and makeup at a K-beauty store, get inspired by unique Korean fashion, and sample classic Korean street food dishes. Don't forget to stop by Myeong-dong Cathedral, a stunning Catholic church built in the Gothic style.

☞ **Getting There:** Take Seoul Subway Line 4 to Myeong-dong Station and go out exit 6 OR take Line 2 and get off at Euljiro 1-ga Station, Exit 5.

HAPJEONG

This trendy up-and-coming neighborhood is popular with Korean hipsters, fashionistas and foodies. It's a younger, cooler crowd with great music and even better people watching. Hapjeong is the perfect spot to take in funky art installations and live music. It's also more of a local spot so you'll find smaller tourist crowds and trendier young Seoulites out for a day of alternative culture.

☞ **Getting There:** Take the Seoul Subway Line 2 or Line 6 and get off at Hapjeong Station; then take Exit 10.

SINSA

This charming neighborhood is perfect for a girl's day out! Stroll down gingko tree-lined streets, sip a fancy latte with foam art, and hit Sinsa's many boutiques and vintage clothing shops. Pick up some sheet masks and top-shelf makeup before lunching at the city's favorite spots for fashionista bloggers. If you want to be super-extra, stop at the Simone Handbag Museum, where you can design your own unique bag.

☞**Getting There:** Get on the Seoul Subway Line 3 to Sinsa Station and take Exit 8.

SONGHYEON-DONG

In the mood for art? Look no further than Songhyeon! This neighborhood is home to Korea's National Museum of Modern and Contemporary Art, as well as a plethora of small galleries run by local Korean artists. Make time to sightsee at Gyeongbok Palace and Jogyesa Temple, and learn more about Korea's traditional art scene at the Songhyeon Dong Cultural Center.

☞ **Getting There:** Located next to Anguk station, subway line 3, exit 1.

South Korea Notes...

....

....

....

....

....

....

....

WHERE TO STAY IN SEOUL

FOUR SEASONS

Have you ever been a princess? This is your chance to be royalty on a commoner's budget. The Four Season Hotel in Seoul is an unforgettable experience that will leave you feeling like a celebrity. Think I'm being dramatic? No, if anything, I'm toning it down. This is the cheapest Four Seasons I've ever found yet the quality of rooms, service, food and prime location do not disappoint. Come see why this hotel is consistently ranked the best in Seoul...starting with their must-try spa complete with plunge jacuzzis...then at their world-famous bar that is often considered one of the best in Asia.

🎟 **Budget:** $$$$$

☆ **Style:** Luxury Resort

♥ **Where:** Steps from Gwanghwamun Plaza and station

🏛 **Address:** Address: 97, Saemunan-ro, Jongno-gu, Jongno-Gu

 BOOK HERE

L'ESCAPE HOTEL

A Parisian escape with a Korean twist, L'Escape Hotel screams glamour. This award-winning boutique hotel was designed by the famous Jacques Garcia who is internationally known for pairing history with comfort in his hotel designs. This hotel represents the nineteenth century period of the Belle Époque in France. Treat yourself to the SPA by BEAUTÉ BR which uses luxurious French aesthetic products in their indulgent treatments. After the hustle and bustle of Seoul, this is the most serene hotel to return to.

Budget: $$$

☆ **Style:** Luxury Resort

♥ **Where:** Steps from Hoehyeon Subway Station

📷 **Address:** 67, Toegye-ro, Jung-gu, Jung-Gu

 BOOK HERE

DORMY INN SEOUL GANGNAM

If you love late-night food, this is your spot - Dormy Inn offers free ramen every night from 9:30-11:00pm! But the food isn't the only thing to love about this hotel. It's in a central location in Gangnam and features a beautiful spa and sauna (Jjimjilbangs) to soak away a day of sightseeing or night of dancing. Wrap it up with a great on-site restaurant and 24-hour, English-speaking front desk staff, and you've got an overall fantastic value!

Budget: $$$

☆ **Style:** Private rooms

♥ **Where:** Three blocks west of Sinnonhyeon Station

📷 **Address:** 134, Bongeunsa-ro, Gangnam-gu, Gangnam-Gu, 06124 Seoul

BOOK HERE

L7 HONGDAE BY LOTTE

Absolute bang for your buck! Stay at a posh hotel with idyllic rooms, fitness center, and glamourous bar and restaurant with taking in the city views. There's even a rooftop pool open during the hotter months (although it does come with a small additional fee). Best of all, you'll also be just steps away from the Hongik University subway stop, putting the entire city essentially at your fingertips!

🎟️ *Budget:* $$

☆ *Style:* private rooms

📍 *Where:* One block east from Hongik University Station Exit 1

🏛 *Address:* 141, Yanghwa-ro, Mapo-gu

BOOK HERE

GLAD GANGNAM COEX CENTER

This sleek modern hotel will have you living the high life in Gangnam! Staying in Gangnam, it is impossible to find a better deal than this. The rooms are quaint but exquisite and clean. The staff go above and beyond to take care of you (you will feel like you are staying with family). And the location does not get any better than this if you're looking to explore Gangnam. Post up at their sexy bar to meet some fellow travelers and then step out the front door into the wild world of Gangnam nightlife. To explore other areas in Seoul, walk one-minute to Samseong Station.

🎟️ *Budget:* $$

☆ *Style:* Private rooms

📍 *Where:* Next to Samseong Station

🏛 *Address:* 610, Teheran-ro, Gangnam-gu, Gangnam-Gu, 06174 Seoul

BOOK HERE

9 BRICK HOTEL

Big ass rooms in central Hongdae with bathtubs at an affordable price! How do they do it?! You'll be in the center of everything from cheap street food to cultural sites to some of the city's best nightlife. Go party like a wild woman but return to your crisp, modern room as a classy lady - 9 Brick Hotel offers the best of both worlds. You're a quick walk to the subway, by the way, which will make exploring Seoul easy-peasy.

🏷️*Budget:* $$

☆ *Style:* Private rooms

📍*Where:* Two blocks east from Hongik University Station

🏠*Address:* 32, Hongik-ro 5-gil, Mapo-gu, Mapo-Gu, 04038 Seoul

 BOOK HERE

SEOUL CUBE ITAEWON

Location is queen at this super convenient, super budget-friendly hostel! Located in the heart of Itaewon, there's no lack of things to do and people to do them with. You'll be just steps away from food, shopping, and nightlife, plus one of Seoul's largest subway stations. Bonus: I love that they have a female-only dorm!

🏷️*Budget:* $

☆ *Style:* Dorm-style

📍*Where:* Across the street from Itaewon Station

🏠*Address:* 8, Usadan-ro 14-gil, Yongsan-gu

 BOOK HERE

INNO HOSTEL & PUB LOUNGE HONGDAE

The social place to stay. Meet your fellow travelers at the on-site bar and restaurant and get sight-seeing recommendations from the friendly, knowledgeable owner and ultra-helpful staff. Inno is in a primo location in Hongdae which is accessible to a ton of attractions, restaurants, shopping, and transportation options. You can't go wrong.

Budget: $

☆ **Style:** Dorm-style and private rooms

Where: Three blocks northwest of Hapjeong Station

Address: 37-7, World Cup-ro 8-gil, Mapo-gu

 BOOK HERE

BINGO HOSTEL INSADONG

Free things are nice, right? Free laundry and free travel essentials make you feel pampered and cared for right off the bat at this small but perfectly-run hostel in one of the quirkiest neighborhoods in Seoul. It's hard to find a clean and cozy private room for this cheap in this city. Take advantage.

Budget: $

☆ **Style:** Small private rooms

Where: Right near the subway

Address: 63-13, Jong-ro, Jongno-gu, Jongno-Gu

 BOOK HERE

ALTERNATIVE OPTION: JJIMJILBANGS

For a truly unique South Korean experience, spend a night in a jjimjilbangs! These popular public saunas are open 24 hours a day and offer sleeping spaces where it's quite common for locals to crash after an evening of relaxation. Get an invigorating full-body scrub, take a luxurious soak in a peaceful hot tub, and hop between hot and cold saunas. Yes, the tubs and saunas are clothing-free but I guarantee after a couple minutes, you'll be so relaxed you won't even notice.

In more traditional jjimjilbangs, the sleeping arrangements are basic - you (and everyone else spending the night!) will get a mat on the floor. Some of the larger and more modern spas have actual beds. Don't let the sleeping arrangements scare you off; they're part of the adventure!

Jjimjilbangs are totally safe - the bathing portions are separated by gender, and there are female-only sleeping areas. They're the perfect way to sweat out some toxins after a night on the town!

Pro Tip: Many jjimjilbangs have day rates and night rates; if you can, wait to check in until the night rate kicks in!

Try: Dragon Hill Spa

This is one of the biggest and most popular jjimjilbangs in Seoul. Try the Crystal Salt Sun Room (just step carefully - the salt pebbles can hurt!) or the traditional Korean charcoal kiln (pile), which comes in three different temperatures. You can also relax in massage chairs or get a body scrub or true massage (which are SO affordable compared to back home).

Don't forget to hit up the snack bar and if you're still not ready for bed, check out the arcade room or karaoke room. When you're ready to turn in, head up to the sixth floor to the female-only sleeping room.

🏷️**Budget:** Budget

☆ **Style:** Dorm style

📍**Where:** To the right from Yongsan Station Exit 1.

🚇**Address:** 40, Hangang-daero 21na gil, Yongsan-gu, Seoul 04378

Pro Tip! You can purchase discounted tickets for Dragon Hill Spa online here...

WHERE TO EAT

Coffee Shops

ANTHRACITE COFFEE HANNAM

This beloved local spot is known for its fabulous coffee and its open, welcoming atmosphere. Plenty of seating means you can post up for an hour or two and people-watch or plan your day's travels or bring you laptop for a little work sesh.

⊘ **Open:** 9am-11pm

♥ **Where:** Mapo-dong

🏫 **Address:** 10, Tojeong-ro 5-gil, Mapo-gu, Seoul

♥ @anthracite_coffee_roasters

NAMUSAIRO

The espresso is a must-try here! If you're not an espresso fan, though, no worries - the fantastically friendly English-speaking baristas are more than happy to walk you through the menu and find your perfect drink. There's charming indoor and outdoor seating, as well as delicious cakes and sweets!

ANTHRACITECOFFEE.COM

Open: 10am-10pm

Where: Jongno, near Four Seasons

Address: 21 Sajik-ro 8-gil, Sajik-dong, Jongno-gu, Seoul

@namusairocoffee

CAFFE THEMSELVES

This three-level coffee shop is wildly popular with Seoul's hipster crowd, thanks to its industrial decor and award-winning baristas. There's an extensive list of drinks, plus food and desserts. **Pro Tip:** Order your coffee to go and you'll get a discount!

Open: 10am-11pm

Where: Jongno

Address: 388 Samil-daero, Gwancheol-dong, Jongno-gu, Seoul

DAELIM CHANGGO

Imagine Brooklyn in Seoul. That is the Seongsu-dong neighborhood home to Daelim Changgo also known as Column Coffee. It's artsy, it's industrial, it's actually an old warehouse that's been conferred into a cafe and art gallery.

Open: 11am-11pm

Where: Seongsu Station (Seoul Subway Line 2), Exit 3.

Address: 78, Seongsui-ro, Seongdong-gu, Seoul

Breakfast & Brunch

ROOT EVERYDAY

Avocado toast fans, rejoice! Root is the place to go in Seoul to get your avocado fix, plus it's got heaps of other healthy menu items to get your day started feeling light and energized!

Open: 11am-8:30pm (closed Mondays)

Where: Itaewon

Address: 26-4 Itaewon-ro 55ga-gil, Hannam-dong, Yongsan-gu

Check them out here:

BUTTERFINGER PANCAKES

If you're feeling something a little less healthy, swing by Butterfinger Pancakes. You can go the traditional pancake route or try something a little more out of the ordinary, like their T-bone steak pancake. If you're brunching with friends and don't mind a sugar coma, maybe try the Giant Alligator: four different kinds of ice cream sandwiched between layers of waffles and topped with jam and whipped cream.

Open: 7am-1am

Where: Gangnam

Address: 11 Seolleung-ro 152-gil, Cheongdam-don

Lunch & Dinner

LOCAL FOOD

GWANGHWAMUN JIP

Local food alert! This small hole-in-the-wall is famous for its kimchi jjigae, or kimchi stew. Order it with egg rolls or an omelet and you've got a lunch that will keep you warm and full for hours!

⊙ **Open:** 9am-10pm

♥ **Where:** Jongno, near Gwanghwamun Station

🚻 **Address:** 12 Saemunan-ro 5-gil, Sajik-dong, Jongno-gu, Seoul

SAMHAE JIP

Located steps from one of Seoul's major stations (Jonggak station), Samhae Jip has been serving up pork wraps (bossam) and grilled oysters for over 35 years. You also get a steaming bowl of spicy pork spine stew (gamjatang) with your order. Come early and be prepared to wait in line - it's worth it!

⊙ **Open:** 10:30am-2am

♥ **Where:** Jongno

🚻 **Address:** 16-15 Supyo-ro 20-gil, Jongno 3(sam)-ga, Jongno-gu, Seoul

JEONJU JUNGANG

Stop here for South Korea's most iconic soul food: bibimbap. Jeonju Jungang spot is a true hidden gem in the heart of Myeong-dong, making it a great local choice to fuel up a mid-shopping spree. Their menu is simple and basic but delicious and easy to order from.

⊙ **Open:** 9:30am-10:30pm

♥ **Where:** Myeong-dong

🚻 **Address:** 21 Myeong-dong 8na-gil, Chungmuro 1(il)-ga, Jung-gu, Seoul

VATOS URBAN TACOS

Fill up on Mexican-Korean fusion at this funky Itaewon favorite! You have to try the kimchi-carnitas fries, and maybe wash them down with a makgeolita (margarita + Korean rice wine).

⊙ **Open:** 11:30am-11pm Sunday-Thursday; 11:30am-12am Friday and Saturday

♥ **Where:** Itaewon

🚻 **Address:** 1 Itaewon-ro 15-gil, Itaewon 1(il)-dong, Yongsan-gu, Seoul

DINNER

853

Throw a stone on any street in Seoul and you'll hit a Korean BBQ of some kind. If you're in the mood for pork BBQ, this tiny spot is one of the best. The menu is limited to pork shoulder and pork belly, but all the meat is super high quality and delicious. The atmosphere is cozy and welcoming, and the server will help you cook it to perfection.

🕐 **Open:** 12pm-11pm

📍 **Where:** Insa-dong

🏛 **Address:** 16 Insadong 12-gil, Gwanhun-dong, Jongno-gu, Seoul

WALKING ON THE CLOUD

If you feel like splurging on a special meal, you can't go wrong with Walking on the Cloud! Located on the 59th floor, this European-style restaurant and bar offers panoramic views and delicious French-Asian fusion food. There's a decent wine list as well.

🕐 **Open:** 11:30am-3pm; 5:30pm-12am

📍 **Where:** Yeouido

🏛 **Address:** 50, 63-ro, Yeongdeungpo-gu, Seoul

DONGIN-DONG

Korean food is known for its taste bud-scorching heat, and this place is no exception! Order the galbijjim (spicy, garlicky braised short ribs) and pair it with their famous pork pancakes or oyster jeon (oysters dipped in egg and fried).

🕐 **Open:** 12pm-10:30pm

📍 **Where:** Gangnam

🏛 **Address:** 511-5, Sinsa-dong, Gangnam-gu | 1F, Samhwa Bulgyo Daehak, Seoul

TOKKIJUNG PROJECT

One of the most famous spots for Japanese-Korean fusion! Order the Curry Udon with cream! You've never had anything like it. And then order the Strawberry Milk Soda. This place is popular so if there is a line (usually a 30 minute - 1 hours wait) …skip it. If there's no line, take your shot and go eat here.

63RESTAURANT.CO.KR

⊘ **Open:** 11:30am - 10:30pm

♀ **Where:** Locations in Hongdae and Gangnam

MYEONGDONG KYOJA

Fresh, house-made noodles and savory dumplings make this a hotspot for both tourists and locals. And you're guaranteed to never leave hungry - you can get complimentary refills of noodles or rice, so eat your heart out!

⊘ **Open:** 10:30am-9:30pm

♀ **Where:** Myeong-dong

🏯 **Address:** 29-1, Myeongdong 10-gil, Jung-gu | Myeongdong Kyoja #1

TOKYO BINGSU

Winter or summer, Koreans love eating Bingsu! A big ball of shaved iced topped with a liquid syrup that is sometimes sweet and sometimes savory. You can go for flavors like mango, pumpkin, match or...tomato. Eat it with a spoon!

⊘ **Open:** 12pm-10pm (closed Mondays)

♀ **Where:** Mapo-dong

🏯 **Address:** 9 Poeun-ro 8-gil, Mangwon-dong, Mapo-gu

THE
Street Food
BUCKET LIST

- ◯ Namdaemun Market
- ◯ Tongin Market
- ◯ Gwangjang Market
- ◯ Noryangjin Fish Market
- ◯ Sindang-dong Tteokbokki Town
- ◯ Seoul Bamdokkaebi Night Market
- ◯ Dongdaemun Night Market
- ◯ Myeongdong Street Food Alley

Street Food

In my opinion, the best way to eat in South Korea is to go straight for the street food! Food stalls and vendors are pretty ubiquitous in Seoul, and it's fun to just follow your nose. Here's a little more info on my favorite street food spots in Seoul:

GWANGJANG MARKET

This market is one of the oldest continuously functioning markets in the country and is the perfect spot to get a complete taste of Korean street food. Try the mayak kimbap, seaweed-wrapped rolls stuffed with vegetables, pickles, and rice but don't be surprised if you wake up the next morning craving more - its name literally means "narcotic rice roll."

Where: 88 Changgyeonggung-ro, Jongno 4(sa)-ga, Jongno-gu, Seoul

Budget: $3-8 on average

MYEONGDONG STREET FOOD ALLEY

Take a break from shopping and join the throngs of tourists and Seoulites on this popular eating street. You can sample loads of fresh fruit juices and try unique Korean creations like fried milk; the market is also known for its grilled lobster! Make sure you try the bungeoppang, sweet red bean-stuffed pastries shaped like fish.

Where: Myeongdong-gil, Myeong-dong, Jung-gu, Seoul

Budget: $5-20

SINDANG-DONG TTEOKBOKKI TOWN

This market is famous for the Korean comfort food tteokbokki, chewy rice cakes in spicy red sauce. You can sample the classic variety or try innovative twists incorporating seafood, vegetables, and even cheese.

Where: 10-18 Dasan-ro 33-gil, Sindang-dong, Jung-gu, Seoul

Budget: $5-10 on average

NORYANGJIN FISH MARKET

Come to Noryangjin if you're in the mood for fresh-off-the-boat seafood! Wander among the vendors, choose your fish or shellfish, and have them prepare it for you at one of the on-site restaurants. Be sure to get some side dishes, like bokkeumbap (fried rice) or maeuntang (spicy fish-based broth).

Where: 674 Nodeul-ro, Noryangjin-dong, Dongjak-gu, Seoul

Budget: Depending on what you buy, seafood ranges from $8 to upwards of $30

Pro Tip: Haggling at Noryangjin is encouraged so have at it!

WHERE TO DRINK

FRIED CHICKEN SPOTS

As I mentioned earlier, fried chicken and beer are a match made in heaven in Korea. Here are a few of my favorite places to partake in this wonderful subsection of Korean drinking culture in Seoul:

◊Brew 3.14

◊Brew 3.15

◊Daily Beer

SANCHEZ MAKGEOLLI

This basement bar oozes with kitschy charm, from its dim lighting to its Santa decor. Sample makgeolli, one of South Korea's most traditional liquors, a milky rice wine that's simultaneously sweet and tangy. They serve great late-night food as well if you need a little something to soak up the booze!

🕑 **Open:** 6pm-1:30am

📍 **Where:** Anguk

🏛 **Address:** 26 Yunposun-gil, Anguk-dong, Jongno-gu, Seoul

MAGPIE BREWING COMPANY

One of the pioneers of Seoul's craft beer scene, Magpie brews a wide range of styles that incorporate local Korean ingredients like Jeju tangerines and hobak pumpkins. They've become especially famous in recent years for their seasonal sours. Magpie has indoor and outdoor seating and the vibe is friendly and casual. Oh, and their brewery dog is pretty damn cute, too!

🕑 **Open:** 3pm-1am

📍 **Where:** Itaewon

🏛 **Address:** 244-1, Noksapyeong-daero, Yongsan-gu, Seoul

BULLDOG PUB

English-speaking staff and friendly crowds make this a great place to start (or end!) a night out in Gangnam. The drink menu is limited but reasonably priced, and regulars can join the shot club - buy 50 different shots and you get your name on a plaque on the wall!

◎ **Open:** 7pm-1am

♀ **Where:** Gangnam

🏛 **Address:** 810-2 Yeoksam-dong, Gangnam-gu, Seoul

ALICE

You'll drop a bit more cash at this swanky cocktail lounge (including a cover charge of about $8) but it's worth the splurge. From the sexy backlit bar to the cozy velvet sofas, the ambience is everything you want in a high-end bar. The cocktails are creative and delicious, as are the bar snacks. Just a head's up - the bathroom doors are camouflaged!

◎ **Open:** 7pm-3am

♀ **Where:** Gangnam

🏛 **Address:** 47, Dosandaero 55-gil, Gangnam-gu, Seoul

LOWER GIN

Gin lovers won't want to miss this adorable little bar in Itaewon. It's located in a flower shop and offers a small but perfectly crafted gin menu. You'll have a great time hanging out with the lovely owner and her friendly dog!

◎ **Open:** 5pm-12am

♀ **Where:** Itaewon

🏛 **Address:** 250 Noksapyeong-daero, Itaewon 2(i)-dong, Yongsan-gu, Seoul

RABBITHOLE ARCADE PUB

For an unforgettable night, stop by the Rabbithole for a drag burlesque show! The drinks are strong and cheap, the bartenders are incredibly friendly, and there are a bunch of retro arcade games to keep you occupied between acts.

◎ **Open:** 8pm-2am Tuesday-Thursday; 8pm-5am Friday and Saturday; closed Sunday and Monday (check their Facebook page for show schedules)

♀ **Where:** Yongsan

🏛 **Address:** 39-17 Yongsandong 2(i)-ga, Yongsan-gu, Seoul, South Korea

THINGS TO DO IN SEOUL

Traveling solo is badass, but sometimes you want to meet some new people and gain a fresh perspective through the eyes of a local!

Go ahead, book a tour or two!

History & Culture

HALF-DAY DMZ TOUR

Peek behind the curtain of the world's most mysterious country at the Korean peninsula's Demilitarized Zone. The DMZ is a strip of uninhabited land that acts as a buffer between North Korea and South Korea. In recent years, it's become an increasingly popular tourist attraction, with guided tours allowing foreign and domestic travelers to get a glimpse of South Korea's enigmatic neighbor. Use the binoculars at one of two observatories to gaze over the border or if you're feeling really adventurous, you can actually stand IN North Korea at the Joint Security Area, a small parcel of land occupied by South Korean and U.S. military.

☆ **Style:** Group

💸 **Budget:** $57

⊘ **How Long:** About 6 hours

BOOK HERE

SEOUL IN ONE DAY

Want to see everything Seoul has to offer but not quite sure where to start? Check out this comprehensive tour! You'll go to 10 of the city's main historic and cultural sights, plus explore some hidden spots that only locals know!

☆ *Style:* Group

✎ *Budget:* $62

◉ *How Long:* 4.5 hours

SOUTH KOREAN COOKING CLASS AND MARKET TOUR

Impress the guests at your next dinner party with homemade Korean food! You'll start at a traditional Korean market, where your guide will introduce you to local ingredients. Then you'll return to her private home, where you'll learn to make three classic Korean dishes.

☆ *Style:* Private

✎ *Budget:* $62

◉ *How Long:* 3 hours

 BOOK HERE

GO ON A FOOD TOUR

Obviously one of the top things (if not the top thing) to do in South Korea is eat! A food tour is a great way to introduce yourself to the best of Korean food. Check out this company that caters specifically to solo travelers.

Pro Tip: Don't skimp on your food tour. Cheap tours are obviously tempting but might not end up being the best experience (think loads of drunk backpackers and stops at super touristy spots); some companies have been known to cancel tours the day of if they haven't booked enough people. Choosing a more expensive tour typically takes away that risk.

RENT A HANBOK

Channel your inner Korean soap opera diva and spend the day strolling around Seoul in a traditional hanbok! These gorgeous outfits consist of a long, high-waisted skirt and a short jacket and come in a dazzling array of colors and patterns to make you feel like a princess. You can rent a hanbok by the hour or for a whole day; some packages include photography to snag that perfect new profile pic.

♥ Where: There's at least one hanbok rental shop at virtually every major tourist attraction. You can also book an appointment online here

How Much: Starting at $7

 BOOK HERE

Free Things

WALK ALONG CHEONGGYECHEON STREAM

Immerse yourself in nature and art along this 7-mile stretch of river running through the heart of the city. The Cheonggyecheon Stream was recently revitalized as part of an urban renewal project and has become a hugely popular place among locals to walk, picnic, and just hang out in the fresh air. Wander under the river's 22 unique bridges and check out Cheonggyecheon Museum. If you're there after sunset, catch the illumination show at Cheonggye Plaza.

Budget:: Free

Where: 530 Cheonggyecheon-ro, Majang-dong, Seongdong-gu

VISIT A FREE MUSEUM

No matter your travel budget, there's nothing better than finding cool free things to do! Some cost-effective museum-hopping is the perfect way to spend a rainy or excessively hot and humid day!

◊Here is a Selection of Wonderful Museums in Seoul:

◊National Museum

◊Agricultural Museum

◊National Folk Museum

◊National Museum of Korean Contemporary History

Budget: Free! Yippee!

GO HIKING

Hiking is pretty close to being South Korea's national sport, and Seoul has some great trails right outside its front door! Bukhansan, Seouraksan, Achasan, and Dobongsan will all give you fabulous views, with varying levels of difficulty. Remember to bring water and snacks!

Fun Things

SING (AND DRINK) IN A NORAEBONG

It's virtually impossible to spend time in South Korea and not find yourself in a noraebang. These private karaoke rooms play an important role in Koreans' social life and culture! You pay for the room by the hour and can order snacks and drinks while you sing your heart out.

Pro Tip: Most noraebangs are completely on the up-and-up but some do feature "helpers" - scantily clad women who get paid to hang out and drink with the customers. These places aren't dangerous but they are a little seedy and creepy. Look for noraebangs that are well-lit and more modern-looking to avoid any sketchiness!

💸*Budget::* Anywhere from $5-$30 an hour

📍*Where:* Try Luxury Su Noraebang in Hongdae or just wander literally every nightlife neighborhood which will have plenty of noraebang options. Just look for a sign that says 노래방.

VISIT LOTTE WORLD

If you're a theme park aficionado, you won't want to miss South Korea's answer to Disney. Lotte World consists of the world's largest indoor amusement park, as well as an outdoor amusement park, shopping malls, restaurants, a movie theater, and a luxury hotel. With almost 40 rides plus seasonal festivals and shows, it's easy to spend a full day here!

💸*Budget:* $50 in the day; $41 after 4pm

📍*Where:* 240 Olympic-ro, Jamsil-dong, Songpa-gu, Seoul

Pro Tip: Think about investing in a Magic Pass to skip the lines!

TAKE A K-POP TOUR

Love BTS and EXO? Book yourself a K-pop tour to visit music video filming locations, K-pop broadcasting studios, and the favorite restaurants and bars and even childhood homes of some of the biggest names in the business.

This is also just a really nice way to get a tour of the city while doing something strange!

Budget: $50

Where: Varies by tour; Gangnam is a frequent stop!

 BOOK HERE

HAVE A REAL GIRL'S NIGHT OUT AT MR. SHOW

Feeling a little more scandalous? Check out this live male revue, the renewed version of the famous Korean "Mr. Show". It's for people dreaming of a fantastic one-night escape - an unforgettable evening that is uniquely Korean!

Budget: Tickets start at around $45.

Where: Myungbo Art Hall, 47 Mareunnae-ro, Jung-gu, Seoul

 BOOK HERE

TAKE PHOTOS IN A PHOTO BOOTH

From traditional black-and-white photo studios over cutting-edge digital booths with very unique sceneries to fun frames with your favorite idols or soccer players, Photo Booths in Korea offer a unique and playful way to capture your memories.

Budget: 3-5$

Where: Basically everywhere

SIGHTSEEING IN SEOUL

Palaces & Temples

SUGUKSA TEMPLE

This stunning gold temple was originally built in the 1400s as a place for members of the royalty to be treated for anxiety, stress, and other mental afflictions. Despite its location in the center of Seoul, Suguksa is still relatively unfrequented by tourists. The temple grounds are amazingly quiet, making Suguksa the perfect spot to step away from the hubbub of the city.

🏷️ *Budget:* Free

🕐 *Open:* 24 hours

🚏 *Address:* 8-5 Seooreung-ro 23-gil, Galhyeon 2(i)-dong, Eunpyeong-gu, Seoul

☞ *Getting There:* Take Seoul Subway Line 6 to Gusan Station and exit through Exit 3. Turn right and walk past the pharmacy and Dunkin Donuts; go straight for about 15 minutes and then take a left into the temple grounds when you see the sign for Suguksa.

JINGWANSA TEMPLE

Jingwansa Temple is located in Bukhansan National Park, making it a great starting point for a hike. Wander among brightly colored temple buildings, including three that survived the Korean War and house cultural artifacts dating back to the 1600s. This temple is the only one in the city that still engages in Suryukje, a Buddhist ceremony that provides food and Buddhist teachings to wandering spirits and starved demons; the ceremony takes place every leap year and goes on for 49 days!

Pro Tip: To really get a taste of Korean temple life, try Jingwansa's temple stay program

🪙 **Budget:** Free

⊙ **Open:** 24 hours

🏛 **Address:** 73 Jingwan-gil, Jingwan-dong, Eunpyeong-gu, Seoul

☞ **Getting There:** Take Seoul Subway Line 3 or Line 6 to Yeonsinnae Station and take exit 3. Make a U-turn outside the exit and then turn right at the corner; you'll see a free shuttle bus one block down that will take you to the temple grounds.

JOGYESA TEMPLE

One of the most important Buddhist temples in South Korea, Jogyesa features the largest temple building in Seoul. The temple is nestled in the center of the city, making it a quick stop to rest from shopping and eating!

🪙 **Budget:** Free

⊙ **Open:** 24 hours

🏛 **Address:** 55 Ujeongguk-ro, Gyeonji-dong, Jongno-gu, Seoul,

☞ **Getting There:** Take Seoul Subway Line 1 to Jonggak Station or Line 3 to Anguk Station. Take Exit 2 from Jonggak or Exit 6 from Anguk.

GYEONGBOKGUNG PALACE

This is the largest and most culturally important of Seoul's five palaces. Gyeongbokgung means "Greatly Blessed by Heaven." The Gwanghwamun Gate and Heungnyemun Gate are particularly iconic and a great spot to snap an impressive picture. You can watch the Changing of the Guard ceremony at the top of every hour from 11am to 3pm, and English-language guided tours are given for free at 11am, 1pm, and 3:30pm. You can also visit the National Folk Museum of Korea and the National Palace Museum of Korea.

🪙 **Budget:** $2.50

⊙ **Open:** 9am-6pm; closed Tuesdays

🏛 **Address:** 161 Sajik-ro, Sejongno, Jongno-gu, Seoul

☞ **Getting There:** Take Seoul Subway Station Line 3 to Gyeongbokgung Station; Exit 5 connects you to the palace directly.

Pro Tip: If you rent a hanbok to wear, you get free admission to Gyeongbukgong!

CHANGDEOKGUNG & CHANGGYEONGGUNG (EAST PALACE COMPLEX)

Don't miss Seoul's most famous UNESCO World Heritage site! The palace grounds are nestled at the foot of Mount Baegaksan, and the architects designed the buildings to blend harmoniously with the surrounding natural landscape. The result is a peaceful sprawling complex of historic buildings and blooming gardens. It's particularly stunning in the spring and fall!

🗂 *Budget:* $2.50

⊙ *Open:* 9am-5pm

🏛 *Address:* 9, Yulgok-ro, Jongno-gu, Seoul 03072

☞ *Getting There:* Take Seoul Subway Line 3 to Anguk subway station and head east from Exit 3.

More Sights to See in Seoul

BANPO BRIDGE

This massive bridge spans the Han River and connects Seocho and Yongsan. The big draw here is the Moonlight Rainbow Fountain Show. Streams of water arc 200 feet into the air illuminated by multi-colored LED lights, all set to music. The show runs from April to October; there are daytime showings but you definitely want to catch it at night for the best view!

🎞*Budget:* Free

🕐 *Open:* M-F: 12pm,, 8pm, 8.30pm and 9pm; Saturday and Sunday: 12pm, 6pm, 7.30pm, 8pm, 8.30pm and 9pm.

🚇 *Address:* Banpo 2(i)-dong, Seoul

☞ *Getting There:* Take Seoul Subway Line 3, 7, or 9 to the Express Bus Terminal Station. Leave from Exit 8-1 and walk straight.

APGUJEONG GRAFFITI TUNNEL

Take in some urban art (and snag some killer Instagram photos!) in the Apgujeong Graffiti Tunnel. This tunnel connects the Apgujeong neighborhood to the Han river and is completely covered with a multitude of colorful murals. It gained its fame from several famous Korean romance movies

🎞*Budget:* Free

🕐 *Open:* 24 hours

🚇 *Address:* Apgujeong-dong, Gangnam-gu, Seoul

☞ *Getting There:* Take the Bundang Line subway to Apgujeongrodeo Station and go through Exit 1. Walk straight out the exit toward the river for about 10 minutes.

NAMSAN PARK

Stretch your legs and get some nature therapy in Namsan Park while you take in panoramic views of the city. The largest park in Seoul, Namsan is home to North Seoul Tower, which rises almost 800 feet above the ground. Check out the Mongmyeoksan Beacon Hill Site, a set of warning beacons set up to warn the city of enemy invasion. If you're feeling romantic, visit the Locks of Love wall where you can hang a lock to memorialize your relationship.

Budget: Free to enter the park; $9 to reach the North Seoul Tower observation deck

⊙ *Open:* The park is open 24 hours; the Tower is open from 10am-11pm on weekdays and 10am-midnight on weekends.

🛏 *Address:* 100-177 Hoehyeon-dong 1-ga, Jung-gu | Yongsan-dong, Yongsan-gu, Seoul

☞ *Getting There:* Take Seoul Subway Line 4 to Myeongdong Station and leave through Exit 3; from there you'll see the Namsan shuttle bus stop.

LEEUM SAMSUNG MUSEUM OF ART

This prestigious museum showcases traditional Korean art as well as contemporary art by both Korean and international artists. Thirty-six pieces in the museum have been designated as Korean national treasures. Go at 3pm on weekends to take an English-language tour.

Budget: $8.50

⊙ *Open:* 10:30am-6pm; closed Mondays

🛏 *Address:* 60-16 Itaewon-ro 55-gil, Hannam-dong, Yongsan-gu, Seoul

☞ *Getting There:* Take Seoul Subway Line 6 to Hangangjin Station. Go through Exit 1 and walk straight until you see a sign for the museum on the right.

SHOPPING IN SEOUL

HONGDAE WALKING STREET

If you only have time to go shopping one time while in South Korea, I recommend you hit the streets of Hongdae. Not only will you find the most affordable high-quality clothing and beauty products, but this is also the best place to go souvenir shopping for cute and quirky gifts to bring home.

📍 **Where:** Hongdae

☞ **Getting There:** Subway Line 2 to Hongik University Station. Exit 9.

COMMON GROUND

I highly recommend you come here! Common Ground is this trendy shopping area (with food and coffee) that is comprised of about 200 shipping containers that house both big brands and one-of-a-kind shops with weird, cute and quirky things that you never knew you needed.

There are restaurants on the third floor, but save your appetite for the food trucks that pull up out front - better food, better prices, and a great way to mingle with the locals!

📍 **Where:** Gwangjin

☞ **Getting There:** Take Seoul Subway Line 2 or 7 and get off at Konkuk Station; go straight out of Exit 6 and walk for about a tenth of a mile.

SEOUL FOLK FLEA MARKET (PUNGMUL FLEA MARKET)

Wander among a seemingly endless line of stalls offering traditional Korean goods and food, souvenirs, antiques, and crafts. The market is separated into color-coded zones; each color represents a different type of goods for sale, from regional specialties to fashion and accessories to art. Like any good flea market, you'll want to take plenty of time to sift through the piles and find your treasures!

📍 **Where:** Sinseoul

☞ **Getting There:** Take Seoul Subway Line 1 to Sinseol-dong Station and leave through Exit 9. Walk straight for about five minutes.

DONGDAEMUN NIGHT MARKET

One of Seoul's most popular tourist attractions, Dongdaemun Night Market is crowded year-round but worth a visit. It's also known as Yellow Tent Market thanks to the dozens of yellow tents that spring up as soon as the sun goes down. From clothes to purses to souvenirs and street food, it has everything you want in a night market!

♀Where: Jongno

☞ **Getting There:** Take Seoul Subway Line 2, 4, or 5 to Dongdaemun History & Culture Park and go through Exit 2 or 3; it's just a few minutes' walk from there.

GAROSU-GIL

This tree-lined street boasts high-end fashion and classy cafes. You won't find smoking deals here but you can do plenty of window-shopping and take in creative fashions from some of Korea's most prestigious up-and-coming designers as well as big international names.

♀Where: Gangnam

☞ **Getting There:** Take Seoul Subway Line 3 to Sinsa Station.

NAMDAEMUN MARKET

Prepare to spend at least a few hours in this sprawling market spanning multiple streets. You can find cheap souvenirs and trinkets, as well as any necessities for your trip you might have forgotten!

♀Where: Junggu

☞ **Getting There:** Take Seoul Subway Line 4 Heoyeon Station and leave through Exit 4, 5, or 6.

Pro Tip: Namdaemun has some restaurants but if you're really in the mood for street food, you'll be better served going to Gwangjang Market.

APGUJEONG RODEO STREET

Welcome to the center of Seoul's fashion universe! From luxury clothes and shoes to designer handbags and world-class hair salons and cosmetics shops, you'll find everything you need for a day of (pricey) pampering.

♀Where: Apgujeong

☞ **Getting There:** Take Seoul Subway Line 3 to Apgujeong Station and go through Exit 3; it's about a 20 minute walk from there. OR Take the Bundang Subway Line to Apgujeong Rodeo Station and take a two minute walk from Exit 6.

Fun Fact!

Blood type is thought to be an indicator of personality and character, so every South Korean knows their blood type.

CHAPTER ONE ──────────────────────────────── SEOUL

CLUBS AND LIVE MUSIC IN SEOUL

ONCE IN A BLUE MOON

Come here for gorgeous jazz plus excellent food and drinks. It's a bit pricey but worth it for a night of good music in a classy but low-key atmosphere! Make a reservation on the weekends.

⊙ **Open:** 6pm-12am Sundays; 6pm-1am Monday-Tuesday; 6pm-2am Wednesday-Saturday

📍 **Where:** Gangnam

🏛 **Address:** 85-1, Chungdam-dong, Gangnam-gu, Seoul

CAKESHOP

This underground club (literally underground, it's in a basement) has made a name for itself with high-quality techno and hip-hop. It won "Best Club in Seoul" in 2018 from 10 Magazine and is always crowded with locals and tourists. The draw here is music and dancing, as opposed to the people-watching at some of the larger clubs. Cover charge runs about $17.

⊙ **Open:** 10pm-5am Thursday-Saturday

📍 **Where:** Itaewon

🏛 **Address:** 134 Itaewon-ro, Itaewon 1(il)-dong, Yongsan-gu, Seoul

NB2

This is one of Hongdae's most famous clubs and for good reason! Owned and operated by YG, a famous South Korean rapper and music producer,

NB2 is the place to be if you're into old-school hip-hop. It's a true club - think loud music and huge crowds - so make sure you're in the mood to mingle! Cover charge will cost you about $12.

🕐 **Open:** 12am-6:30am

📍**Where:** Mapo

🏛 **Address:** 72 Wausan-ro, Mapo-gu, Seoul

OCTAGON

Gangnam's most famous clubs. It's the place to see and be seen for elite young Seoulites...but they are not very welcoming to foreigners, especially since the pandemic hit. You may be denied entry. But hey, if you get in, message me on Instagram and let me know about your experience.

🕐 **Open:** 12am-8am Thursday-Sunday; closed Monday-Wednesday

South Korea Notes...

Hey...

YOU CAN TOTALLY DO THIS.

I PROMISE.

Nervous about going to South Korea?

Reach out to me via email.

I'll give you a little pep talk...
alexa@alexa-west.com

CHAPTER TWO

Busan

—

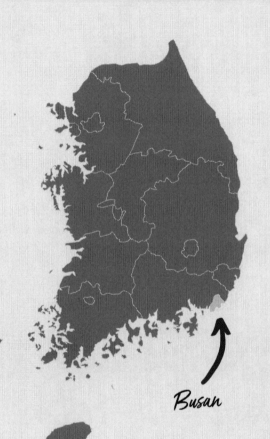

Busan

INTRODUCTION
TO BUSAN

The most vibrant port city for seafood, nightlife, and beaches, and where I lived for one blissful year of my life!

Much smaller than Seoul, Busan is easy to navigate by subway and easy to wander into more local pockets of life. Chill at the beach, go shopping in the underground subways, hang out with college students in the University district, go hiking in the hills or head over to the biggest fish market in Korea, Jagalchi. The ninth-busiest port in the entire world, Busan is a thriving cultural and social hub!

The city is also of huge historical importance to South Korea - it served as the country's temporary capital during the Korean War. Immerse yourself in the city's history, culture, and art at Busan's dozens of museums. Take in breathtaking and one-of-a-kind temples, and enjoy spectacular city and ocean views from one of the city's surrounding peaks.

With so much to offer, it's easy to see why most English teachers strive to land a coveted job in Busan! When you come here, expect to mingle with expats from all over the world. It's easy to make some new friends to eat street food with and end the night at an expat bar or noraebang.

Fun Fact!

Lunar New Year is South Korea's biggest holiday of the year; many South Koreans travel to their hometown to spend time with their families.

Getting there from Seoul

By Train

In my opinion, the best option for getting from Seoul is on the KTX train. It's faster than a bus and less expensive than a plane, and it's pretty comfortable! This high-speed train will get you to Busan in about 3 hours (not counting the time to transfer from Incheon Airport).

🕐 **When:** KTX trains run from Seoul Station approximately every 20 minutes from 5am-10:30pm. There is typically no need to book in advance unless it's a public Korean holiday.

📍 **Where:** If you're coming straight from Incheon Airport, you'll take either the subway or the AREX Airport express train to Seoul Station (see the Seoul chapter for info on where to catch these trains!). This will take you about an hour. Once you reach Seoul Station, head to the ground floor, look for the KTX information desk and ticket kiosks.

💵 **How Much:** $40-50 for the KTX, plus the cost of transfer to Seoul Station if needed

By Bus

Your least expensive option to get from Seoul to Busan is by bus. There's also a direct connection from Incheon Airport, cutting out the need to transfer to Seoul Station if you're coming straight from the airport. The trip by bus will take you about five hours, depending on traffic; you'll go either to Nopo Bus Terminal (the official name of it is Busan Dongbu Bus Terminal) which is on the last stop of Busan Subway Line 1 (about an hour outside the center of the city by subway) or Haeundae Bus Station.

🕐 **When:** The Haeundae Station bus runs three times per day, while the Nopo Bus Terminal, (the official name of it is Busan Dongbu Bus Terminal)

route runs every 90-120 minutes. Buses run from around 6:30am-11:30pm.

♀ Where: At Incheon Airport: Head to the ticket counters inside the arrivals terminal, to the right of Gate B or to the left of Gate D. There are also outdoor counters next to Exits 4, 6, 7, 8, 11, and 13. Your ticket will contain information on which bus stop is yours.

From Seoul (not the airport)

Take Subway Line 3, 7, or 9 to the Express Bus Terminal and look for the Gyeongbu Bus Terminal; you can buy your ticket and get on the bus from there.

⛟ How Much: The bus will cost around $37 (not counting transfer from Nopo/Haeundae Station).

....

By Plane

Your fastest but most expensive option is to fly from Seoul to Busan. Domestic flights in South Korea go through Gimpo Airport, not Incheon. You can reach Gimpo from Seoul Station by subway in about 20 minutes.

☉ When: Trains run from Seoul Station about every 10 minutes.

♀ Where: Hop on Subway Line 1 or 4, or the Gyeongui-Jungang Line or the Airport Express Line, at Seoul Station to the Seoul Gimpo Airport (GMP) stop.

⛟ How Much: $2.50-3 for a subway ticket; flights will cost anywhere from $50-$200 depending on the time of year.

✈FROM GIMHAE AIRPORT (BUSAN)

By Train

If you fly into Busan, you'll come into Gimhae Airport, which is about 7 miles outside of the city center. The best way to make the transfer unless you arrive late at night or have a lot of luggage is to hop on the subway. It's easy to connect from the airport straight to several major stations!

Follow signs for the subway (you'll be at the Gonghang Station) and get on the Busan-Gimhae light rail transit (BGL) toward Sasang Station. From Sasang, transfer to Busan Subway Line 2 to Seomyeon Station. At Seomyeon, you'll either stay on Line 2 to Haeundae and Gwangali or transfer to Line 1 to get to Busan Station or Nampo.

⊙ **When:** The Busan Subway runs from about 5am-midnight.

♀ **Where:** Follow the signs for the subway (it's in the domestic terminal) and you'll find ticket kiosks and counters as well as station maps and directions to your platform.

💵 **How Much:** No more than $1.5 (1600 won)

....

By Bus

You can also take the airport limousine bus from Gimhae to Busan. It will take you slightly longer depending on traffic but is just as cost-effective as the train.

⊙ **When:** Buses run every 40 minutes or so from 7am to 9:30pm

♀ **Where:** In the domestic terminal, head to the first floor and go out Exit 3; you'll see the bus ticketing counter to your right. When you buy your ticket, proceed to Platform 2; Bus 1 goes to Haeundae and Bus 2 goes to Seomyeon/Busan Station.

💵 **How Much:** $5-7

....

By Taxi/Private Car

If you arrive at Gimhae late at night, have a lot of luggage, or just don't feel like dealing with public transportation, it's easy to grab a cab or a private car. It's obviously more expensive but let's be honest - sometimes convenience is worth the splurge!

⊙ **When:** Pretty much 24 hours a day

♀ **Where:** From the arrivals area, head outside and go to stops 5C-8C. You'll see fleets of cabs waiting for you. If you're taking a private car service, you will get information when you book regarding where to meet your ride, but it will typically be at 3C, 4C, or 13C.

💵 **How Much:** $50-100 depending on your final destination.

Getting around Busan

By Subway

To get around Busan day-to-day, you'll depend mostly on the subway, which is convenient and cost-effective. The Busan Subway Line is the major line; the other important one to know is the Airport Express Line if you are flying in or out of the city at all.

◇ Major Stations:

◇ Busan Station

◇ Haeundae Station

◇ Nampo Station

◇ Seomyeon Station

◇ Gwangan Station

◇ Centum City Station

☉ **When:** $1.25-3 depending on where you're going

Pro Tip: Look into the Busan all-day unlimited metro pass! This will give you unlimited subway rides on the Busan Subway Line on the day of purchase for about $3.75. You can buy this pass inside the subway station.

By Bus

Busan's bus system is extensive and convenient; you can use buses to get to some tourist attractions that aren't easily accessible from a subway station. There are regular city buses (blue and white), express city buses (red and white), and night buses. When you're on the bus, push the button to let the driver know you want to get off and then exit through the back of the bus.

🏷 **How Much:** $1-2

By Taxi

Taxis within Busan are relatively affordable compared to other major cities so they're a good option if you don't want to deal with the crowds or wait for public transport or if you're headed somewhere not accessible by subway or train. You can flag regular taxis at taxi stands at any major station, tourist attraction, or hotel, or just on the street. Just extend your arm with your hand palm down and motion toward yourself. Available taxis will have a red light on their roof or inside the windshield on the passenger side.

How Much: Fares for regular taxis start at $1.50 and go up by about $.10 increments. There is a 20% increase in the base fare at night.

Pro Tip: Try to have the address and name of your destination written out in Korean to make it easier to communicate with the driver.

Walking

Once you're off the subway, each neighborhood is pretty damn explorable by foot! But you'll have to take transportation to get between each neighborhood.

NEIGHBORHOODS TO KNOW IN BUSAN

HAEUNDAE

Between its famous beaches and its lively nightlife, Haeundae rarely sleeps. It's also one of the most foreigner-friendly neighborhoods in this famously foreigner-loving city. You'll find a ton of western bars and restaurants, English signs and English-speaking staff, and fellow travelers.

In the summer months, Haeundae hosts a number of fun festivals, from the Haeundae Sand Festival celebrating wild sand art (and wilder nightly beach parties) to the Busan Sea Festival, filled with street food, water sports, and giant water guns. And if you want to escape some of the crowds, you can head to the eastern edge of the city to Dalmaji Hills, home to a ton of unique art galleries and cozy cafes.

However, choose your hotel carefully because Haeundae is a big city that is spread out. In the "Where to Stay in Busan" section, you can trust that my picks are the most convenient.

CENTUM CITY

Welcome to the center of Busan's shopping world! At one point, the Shinsegae Mall at Centum City held the Guinness Book of World Records title as the largest department store in the world. Once you've loaded up on Korean skincare, fashion and food (one of the best food courts in Korea is here), make your way to the Busan Museum of Art for a little more high-end (and free!) culture - the outdoor sculpture garden is a favorite in good weather.

GWANGALLI

For a slightly more low-key beach experience, head to Gwangalli (sometimes called Gwangan). This beach area is more popular with the locals but still has a foreigner-friendly attitude. It's the heart of Busan's thriving craft beer scene and the home of the Gwangan Bridge, one of Busan's most iconic landmarks. Gwangali Beach is located in the city center, meaning that staying here gives you beach access and access to the subway system to explore the other neighborhoods.

SEOMYEON

Seomyeon is the landlocked hipster neighborhood with a thriving industrial industry, shopping culture and nightlight scene. There is so much to see and do here that I often made it a weekend visit just to walk around and get lost. Wander to shop at trendy Korean boutiques and department stores and or head to Jeonpo Cafe Street to sip on latte art galore.

NAMPO

Nampo is Busan's street food heaven! Start at Jagalchi Fish market, the largest market of its kind in the country, and then wander through BIFF Square tasting every sort of Korean delicacy under the sun. Wrap up your day with a visit to the charming Bosu-dong Book Street to pick up a new read for your flight home.

PUSAN NATIONAL UNIVERSITY (PNU)

Located around Busan's major university, this area is known for its cheap eats and fun nightlife. PNU was basically ground zero for the massive influx of English teachers in the 1990s and the area is still super popular with expats and travelers. You can catch great live music here as well, and the neighborhood is a bit more low-key than other nightlife spots like Haeundae.

WHERE TO STAY IN BUSAN

BEOMEOSA TEMPLE STAY

Sleep at a Buddhist temple as the Buddhist monks do. Wake up early, eat what they eat, meditate how they meditate and get a unique look into the life of a monk. Make sure you read the etiquette section of this experience to see if you're up for being on your cleanest behavior (both spiritually and mater-of-factually). When you arrive, you will trade in your clothes for temples clothes and your busy life for a season of peace.

📍 **Where:** Beomeosa Temple

🎫 **Budget:** $$

 BOOK HERE

PARADISE HOTEL BUSAN

The big hotel with multiple pools, views of the ocean and a location right at the footsteps of Haeundae Beach. If you've come to party or just relax under the sun for days on end, this is where you want to come. They've got a spa, a beach bar and breakfast that is to die for. I highly recommend splurging and getting a room with a balcony that overlooks the ocean!

💵 *Budget:*$$$$

☆*Style:* Private rooms

📍 *Where:* Just steps to Haeundae Beach!

🏨*Address:* 296, Haeundaehaebyeon-ro

 BOOK HERE

ANANTI HILTON BUSAN

Yes, it's pricey but man, do they make every dollar count! Take in jaw-dropping views from a rooftop infinity pool overlooking the ocean - and that's just one of five pools to enjoy on property. If that's not enough to get you here, the Hilton Busan features an unbelievably swanky restaurant and a sexy rooftop lounge, an enormous modern fitness center with an ocean view, and a relaxing sauna and sun deck. The Hilton is a bit outside of Busan proper, but there is plenty of gorgeous scenery and walking trails to take in - if you ever want to leave the hotel, that is.

💵 *Budget:* $$$

☆*Style:* Private rooms

📍 *Where:* Quiet seafront, 5-minute taxi to Haeundae Beach

🏨*Address:* 268-32, Gijanghaean-ro, Gijang-eup

 BOOK HERE

NAMPO HOUND HOTEL PREMIER

This location is super central! Kick back after a long day of shopping, sightseeing, and eating on the Nampo Hound's gorgeous rooftop bar and terrace lounge, or take a nice long soak in your room's luxurious soaking tub. And luxury isn't all Nampo Hound has to offer. This location puts you close to Jagalchi fish market and a ton of transportation options, including the subway, so you can get lost and wander (which I recommend).

💵 *Budget:* $$
☆*Style:* Private rooms
📍 *Where:* Smack dab in the middle of Nampo-dong's best sights
🏨*Address:* 24, Bosu-daero, Jung-gu

 BOOK HERE

BROWN DOT HOTEL SEOMYEON

Chic rooms with big bathtubs and sparkling city views - you'll be pampered in the center of it all at the Brown Dot. The restaurant terrace has a fun industrial vibe with exposed brick walls, and it even has a miniature golf putting green. The staff is friendly and check-in times are more flexible than some other places, making this a good choice if you're getting in late at night.

💵 *Budget:* $$
☆*Style:* Private rooms
📍 *Where:* Central Seomyeon
🏨*Address:* 30, Seojeon-ro 9beon-gil, Busanjin-gu

 BOOK HERE

HOTEL HYGGELIG

It's all about the rooftop, baby! Spoil yourself without totally breaking the bank at this gorgeous hotel right on the water. This is one of the cheapest rooms you can find that has an ocean view. There's a fantastic rooftop bar, of course overlooking the ocean, and you're close to some of Haeundae's top restaurants.

Budget: $$

Style: Private rooms

Where: Throw a rock and hit Haeundae Beach!

Address: 28, Dalmaji-gil 62beon-gil

 BOOK HERE

GRAY 193 HOTEL

Four-star amenities for a two-star price! This hotel is just steps from Gwangali Beach, offering stunning water and bridge views. The staff are accommodating and helpful, and the rooms are enormous (for Asia). Enjoy a meal at the on-site restaurant or order room service while you catch up on some Korean dramas!

Budget: $$

Style: Private rooms

Where: Less than a block from Gwangali Beach

Address: B501, 42 Gwanganhaebyeon-ro 278, Suyeong-gu

 BOOK HERE

GUEST HOUSE DEAR MOON

Please stay here at least for one night so that you can go and explore Jagalchi market! This is a truly local experience you cannot miss out on! Before and after the market, you get to snuggle into the coziest dorm beds in the city You can't beat this price or location! Plus, it's clean, safe and the staff are extremely helpful, making your solo trip a breeze.

Budget: $

Style: Dorms

Where: Jagalchi Market

Address: 14-2, BIFF gwangjang-ro, Jung-gu

MAMA GUESTHOUSE HAEUNDAE

Stay at this uber friendly guesthouse and you'll be just steps away from the food heaven of Busan Market, plus just a few minutes from the beach by bus (super easy). The owners are a lovely couple and more than happy to help with recommendations or just to chat. Enjoy a delicious continental breakfast in the charming shared kitchen/lounge space and plan your day with your fellow travelers!

💸 **Budget:** $

⭐ **Style:** Private Rooms

📍 **Where:** Near Haeundae Market

🏠 **Address:** 40, Jungdong 1-ro, Haeundae-gu

 BOOK HERE

South Korea Notes...

....

....

....

....

....

....

....

WHERE TO EAT IN BUSAN

Coffee Shops

BROWN HANDS DESIGN CAFÉ

Located right near Busan Station, the city's major subway stop, this is the place to fuel up for your day. The cafe is in the former location of an old private hospital and has kept some of the building's original features, giving it a spooky yet hipster vibe.

⊘ **Open:** 10am-11pm

♀ **Where:** Choryang

🏫 **Address:** 16 Jungang-daero 209beon-gil, Choryang-dong, Dong-gu Busan, South Korea

BEFORE SUNSET

For truly Instagrammable lattes and desserts, check out this adorable cafe in Seomyeon. Everything is made in-house and its menu changes with the seasons. It also has two equally charming sister cafes: Before Sunrise and Eternal Sunshine.

⊘ **Open:** 12pm-11pm

♀ **Where:** Seomyeon

🏫 **Address:** 690-2 Jeonpo-dong, Busanjin-gu Busan

Fun Fact!

Just about every restaurant in South Korea delivers - even McDonalds.

Breakfast & Brunch

SINCHANG TOAST

Everything on this small menu is delicious, but the real draw? The restaurant opens at 7am! It's rare to find a breakfast spot open in South Korea at what we westerners consider breakfast time, so this is a big win!

⊘ **Open:** 7am-8pm

♀ **Where:** Sinchang

🏠**Address:** 21-1 Gwangbok-ro 39beon-gil, Jung-gu, Busan

ECOTOPIA

Vegetarians, rejoice! This fabulous restaurant offers all vegetarian (and even some vegan!) fare made with the freshest local ingredients. When I say fresh, I mean fresh - some of the produce is even grown on site.

⊘ **Open:** 10am-9pm; closed Mondays

♀ **Where:** Namcheon (not far from Gwangali Beach)

🏠**Address:** 30-6 Suyeong-ro 408 (sabaekpal) beon, Namcheon-dong

BRUNCH CAFE EAN

Stop at this charming cafe in an old Korean-style home for eggs benedict, crepes, waffles, or homemade yogurt. You can't go wrong with their humongous pizza, either!

⊘ **Open:** 11am-11pm

♀ **Where:** Near Gwangali Beach

🏠**Address:** 35-33 Namcheon-dong, Suyeong-gu, Seo-gu, Busan

OBOK RESTAURANT

For a more traditional Korean breakfast, swing by OBok and fill up on a steaming bowl of hearty pork stew with all the fixings! The restaurant is owned by Americans of Korean descent, meaning there is English on the menu, and it's open 24 hours a day!

⊘ **Open:** 24 hours

♀ **Where:** Haeundae

🏠**Address:** 15, Gunam-ro, Haeundae-gu, Busan

Lunch

CHORYANG MILMYEON

Gorgeous cold noodles in spicy broth and gigantic steamed dumplings are the draws to this popular spot near Busan Station. Pair it with perfect kimchi and you'll see why there's almost always a line here.

Open: 10am-10pm

Where: Nampo

Address: 225 Jungang-daero, Choryang-dong, Dong-gu, Busan

JANG SU SAM

This traditional Korean shop has mouth-watering chicken and ginseng stew (samgyetang) that's just perfect on a chilly day. The owner is a sweet lady who will walk you through how to properly eat the soup and tell you about all the delicious banchan! Slip off your shoes, settle onto the comfy mats, and be prepared to leave stuffed.

Open: 11am-8pm

Where: Inland Gwangali area

Address: 7, Suyeongseong-ro 3beon-gil, Suyeong-gu 1f, Busan

NAMASTE HAEUNDAE

Need a break from kimchi? Change it up with some authentic Indian or Nepali food at Namaste Haeundae. The portions here are enormous, and they also have a good selection of halal food.

Open: 11am-11pm

Where: Haeundae

Address: 7, Haeundaehaebyeon-ro 265beon-gil,

THE PARTY

If you're feeling extra hungry after a night of partying (or need to fuel up for one!), check out this popular buffet spot. It's a little pricey, but there's a huge selection of delicious international and Korean food. Get ready to eat your heart out! There are several branches in Busan; I love the one in Haeundae.

Open: M-F 12pm-9pm; Sat 11:30am-9:30pm; Sun 11:30am-8:30pm

Where: Haeundae

Address: 24, Haeundaehaebyeon-ro 298beon-gil, Haeundae-gu B1

Dinner

AN GA

If you've been searching for the best pork BBQ in South Korea, your search is over. An Ga is a constant favorite among locals and tourists alike, and after one bite, you'll know why. High-quality pork in every form imaginable: spare ribs, belly, shoulder, neck, you name it! All served with a delicious choice of sauces and side dishes and of course, washed down with soju. The staff are incredibly friendly and will help make sure your meal is cooked to absolute perfection.

◷ Open: 11:30am-midnight; closed Mondays

♀ Where: Haeundae

🏠 Address: 494-1, Jwadongsunhwan-ro, Haeundae-gu, Busan

MERCIEL

For a more upscale dining experience, throw on some heels and make reservations at this seaside French bistro. The service is impeccable, the wine list is stellar, and the desserts are decadent. Fair warning: your wallet will be lighter.

◷ Open: 12pm-10pm

♀ Where: Haeundae

🏠 Address: 154 Dalmaji-gil 65beon-gil

THE BAY 101

Another option for a splurge-y evening is The Bay 101 Yacht Club. This hotspot at the end of Haeundae Beach is one of the best places in the city to see and be seen while enjoying beautiful views and swanky cocktails. There are multiple seaside dining options, and you can even take a champagne harbor cruise.

◷ Open: 9am-midnight

♀ Where: Haeundae

🏠 Address: 52 Dongbaek-ro, U-dong, Haeundae-gu, Busan

GAEMIJIP

Come here for local seafood delicacies, but be prepared for spiciness! The stir-fried small octopus and octopus stew are two of their most popular dishes. The shop is small so it gets crowded but that just adds to the local flavor!

◷ Open: 11am-10pm

♀ Where: Nampo

🏠 Address: 11-13 Donggwang-dong 2-ga, Jung-gu, Busan

Street Food

All the restaurants above are great. But Busan's real culinary gem is street food! You'll get cheap, delicious eats while taking in Korea's unique street market culture. Here are some of the best food streets in Busan!

JAGALCHI FISH MARKET

For many people, Jagalchi is the definition of Busan street food. This huge fish market is the largest of its kind in South Korea. Wander through row upon row of fresh mussels, crab, lobster, octopus, prawn, and every kind of fish under the sun. When you've worked up an appetite, stop at one of dozens of food stalls and restaurants; you can even buy seafood from one of the vendors and have it cooked right in front of you.

Pro Tip: You'll definitely want to take pictures but try not to stand directly in front of a stall when you do so; you'll block their view of potential customers and they won't be pleased!

♀ Where: Nampo

☞ **Getting There:** Take Busan Subway Line 1 to Jagalchi Station. Go through Exit 10 and then take the second street on your right.

GWANGBOKDONG FOOD STREET

Narrow, crowded, and teeming with sights and smells - Gwangbokdong is everything you want a street food market to be! You'll mingle with lots of locals queuing up for their favorite snacks, including kimbap and ssiat hotteok, but the vendors are pros - before you know it, you'll be handing over your money and walking away with a steaming bowl of whatever your heart desires!

♀ Where: Nampo

☞ **Getting There:** Hop on Busan Subway Line 1 to Jagalchi Station, take Exit 7, and turn down the first street on your left.

GUKJE MARKET FOOD STREET

This open air market has been around for over 60 years and is always bustling with activity. Pull up a plastic stool and enjoy steaming hot pajeon, sundae, and countless other delicacies! Gukje Market is also super convenient to a lot of other attractions

in Nampo, making it an easy place to stop off for lunch or a quick snack while sightseeing!

♀ Where: Nampo

☞ **Getting There:** Take Busan Subway Line 1 to Jagalchi Station and take Exit 7. Turn left at the second road and go straight past BIFF Square.

SEOMYEON FOOD ALLEY

If you haven't fallen in love with Korean food yet, you will after an hour strolling down this famous Busan food street. Lined with pojangmachas (basically a food tent on wheels) serving up everything from fish cakes to tteokbokki to waffles loaded with ice cream and jam, you'll find something to delight your taste buds no matter what you're in the mood for. This is also a popular place for a food tour!

♀ Where: Seomyeon

☞ **Getting There:** Take the subway to Seomyeon Station. Go straight through Exit 1 and turn right down the alley by Starbucks. Food Alley will be down on the left-hand side.

BIFF SQUARE

BIFF Square is famous for the Busan International Film Festival but it's also one of the best places in the city to sample South Korea's famous street fare. It's of course got all the classics, but there are also some unique vendors selling things like garibi (grilled scallops with corn, scallions, and melted cheese) and roasted marshmallows stuffed with ice cream. For the truly adventurous, there's also beondegi - fried silkworm larvae!

📍 **Where:** Nampo

☞ **Getting There:** Take Busan Subway Line 1 to Jagalchi Station and take Exit 7. Turn left at the second road and BIFF Square will be straight ahead.

Fun Fact!

When you reach the age of 60, it's tradition for your family to throw you a huge bash called a hwangap.

WHERE TO DRINK IN BUSAN

GALMEGI BREWING

One of the original craft breweries in Busan, Galmegi Brewing has since opened multiple locations and has gained a cult following both for its stellar western-style burgers and its unique and tasty beers.

⊘ **Open:** Varied by location but generally 5 or 6pm to 1am on weekdays and 3 or 4pm to 2am on weekends

♥ **Where:** Nampo, Haeundae, Seomyeon, and Busan University area

PAPA'S BAR (AKA HAEUNDAE STANDARD)

For some of the best cocktails Haeundae's party scene has to offer, stop by Papa's! The menu is huge and the bartenders really know their stuff and are happy to give recommendations or make a completely customized drink. The whiskey cocktails are particularly strong and delicious!

⊘ **Open:** 8pm-6am

♥ **Where:** Haeundae

🚇 **Address:** 287 Haeundaehaebyeon-ro, Haeundae-gu, Busan

FUZZY NAVEL

After a day lounging on the beach, stroll into the Fuzzy Navel for some cocktails and pub food with a water view. It's got a casual, divey feel and friendly staff and clientele. There's also a good selection of craft beer - the local peach beer is always a hit!

⊘ **Open:** 11am-5am

♥ **Where:** Haeundae

🏛**Address:** 43-1 Gunam-ro, Jung-dong, Haeundae-gu, Busan

THURSDAY PARTY

The name says it all - come here if you want a true party! Loud music, fun young crowds of locals and expats, and strong, cheap drinks. You can even play beer pong! There are three locations: Haeundae, Gwangali, and Seomyeon.

⊘ **Open:** 6pm-4am

♥ **Where:** Haeundae, Gwangali, and Seomyeon

HAPPY MONK

For a quieter night that still has a great crowd and beautiful view, check out Happy Monk in Gwangali. They've got decently priced cocktails and bar bites and are convenient to the other party spots along Gwangali Beach.

⊘ **Open:** M-Thu 5pm-3am; Fri 5pm-5am; Sat 2pm-5am; Sun 2pm-3am

♥ **Where:** Gwangali

🏛**Address:** 187, Gwanganhaebyeon-ro, Suyeong-gu, Busan

Remember...Keep your wits about you when drinking. It's so easy to get carried away in the Korean drinking culture. Especially when Koreans invite you to drink with them. They are much more experienced than you'll ever be...watch your limits.

THINGS TO DO IN BUSAN

There is SO much to do in Busan that it can get overwhelming so first, let me give you a bucket list to help you create your itinerary (ps. there are full itineraries at the end of this book!)

Top 5 Things to Do in Busan

1. SPEND A DAY AT SPA LAND

One of South Korea's largest and most famous jjimjilbangs, Spa Land needs to be on your Busan itinerary! It's located in Shinsegae Centum City, so it's a quick hop, skip, and a jump from the subway. The facility has 22 spas fed by natural spring water, plus 13 themed saunas, and a huge foot spa. Try the Himalayan Salt Room, the Pyramid Room, or the Wave Dream Room! The spa is open from 6am to midnight and one ticket lets you stay for up to four hours.

📎 **Budget:** About $10 on weekdays and $12 on weekends

📍 **Where:** Centum City

More Details Here...

2. BEACH-HOP

Swathes of soft white sand, blue-green water, views for miles, and of course, fireworks - Busan's beaches have it all!

Haeundae Beach tends to be livelier in the summer with volleyball games, snack vendors, musical artist and more people on the beach in general. Gwangalli Beach is that...minus 25% of the vibrancy and busy-ness. Bring a towel, snacks and drinks (yes, you can drink in public here) and enjoy a day watching people on one of these beaches. When you're done, both beaches are lined with bars and restaurants that don't mind if you're a little sandy.

Alternatively, you can head to laid-back cafes of Songdo Beach and the secluded picnic spots of Dadaepo. If you go to Songdo, make sure to hit the skywalk or take the cable car for a sweeping view of the city and the bay.

3. ATTEND A BASEBALL GAME

Even if you're not a sports fan, a South Korean baseball game is a once-in-a-lifetime experience you won't want to miss. Where else can you experience acrobatic first pitches, crazy inflatable clappers, tens of thousands of sports fans wearing plastic bag pom-poms on their heads (yes, I'm serious) and doing choreographed dances? If anything, come for the snacks - from pizza topped with bulgogi to shrimp chips to the ubiquitous fried chicken and beer (chimaek).

I prefer to buy reasonably-priced mini coolers of beer and snacks from the ajummas (grandmas) outside the stadium. However, you can bring your own food, too. Either way, keep your eyes peeled for families camping out with full-on multi-course feasts while watching the game.

You can watch the Lotte Giants at Sajik Stadium from March through September-October.

✒**Budget:** Affordable! Tickets are around $10 and drinks and snacks are totally reasonable, so you can make it a night for less than $30.

♥ **Where:** Dongnae

Book and See the Schedule Here...

4. WANDER GAMCHEON CULTURE VILLAGE

The narrow, winding alleys of this former slum-turned-vibrant cultural hub is filled with endless surprises and treasures. The neighborhood is made up of pastel-painted buildings nestled into the side of a mountain and features street art, food, and history. Stop first at the Haneul Maru Tourist Information Center and Observatory where you'll pick up a map that points out eight designated attractions where you can collect stamps; return all eight to the tourist center on your way out and you'll get a prize!

✍*Budget:* Free to walk around; about $1.75 for a stamp map

☞ *Getting There:* Take Busan Subway Line 1 to Toseong Station; walk out of Exit 6 and then turn right. There will be a small bus station in front of the Pusan National University Hospital building; get on the bus marked Gamcheon Culture Village.

5. VISIT JAGALCHI MARKET

The biggest fish market of its kind where fishermen pull their catch straight out from the sea and either they sell it themselves, their wives are waiting to sell it themselves or they sell it directly to the restaurants which cook you up some of the freshest seafood you've ever had.

Wander. Have some beers. Use the phrase "Mwo ye yo" (what is that) a bazillion times while asking the vendors to introduce you to their sea creatures and eat.

☞ *Getting There:* Take Busan Subway Line 1 to Jagalchi Market and take Exit 7. Take the second road on your left.

More Totally-Worth-It Things to Do in Busan

TAKE A FULL TOUR OF BUSAN

The fastest and smoothest way to experience Busan in one bite! If you're moving to Busan and want to absorb the city quickly or if you just have a few days and don't want to miss the best of Busan, this tour will do it. This cultural tour will take you to some of Busan's most important sites and your guide will give you some insider tips on the city.

🏷️ **Budget:** $42

⭐ **Style:** Private

🕐 **How Long:** Full-day

TAKE A DAY TRIP TO GEOJE ISLAND

Experience a more rural side of South Korea on nearby Geoje Island. This beautiful spot is known for its stunning natural coastline and delicious fresh seafood. It's also home to the largest shipyard in the world, meaning it has a hopping expat scene. From Geoje, you can also hop on a quick ferry to Oedo Island, a gorgeous private island-turned botanical garden.

🏷️ **Budget:** $8-20 depending on packageUsually around $7

☞ **Getting there:** Take a bus.

📍 **Which Station:** Depending on which is closest to you, you can catch a bus at Busan Sasang Bus Terminal (1.2 hour trip), Busan Seobu Intercity Bus Terminal (1.5 hour trip) or Busan Central Bus Terminal (2 hour trip).

🕐 **When:** Google the bus terminal closest to you + Goeje and you'll have a list of times!

How to Buy a Ticket: I prefer to show up at the terminal (use but if it's a weekend or holiday, buy your ticket online.

Remember this article for booking bus tickets like a pro...

DRESS IN HANBOK

Step back in time as you walk through Gamcheon Culture Village in a gorgeous traditional hanbok. You'll get accessories and hairstyle, and you can opt for a package with a professional photo shoot. And before you ask, no, Koreans don't consider this cultural appropriation. You're good to dress up.

💸*Budget:* $8-20 depending on package

☆*Style:* Private

☞ *Book Here...*

WANDER BOSU-DONG BOOK ALLEY

If you're a bibliophile, you've just found heaven! This charming stretch of road in Nampo is filled to the brim with used bookstores. You can get lost for hours just searching for your next great read.

💸*Budget:* Free to walk around

☞*Getting There:* Take Busan Subway Line 1 to Toseong Station and leave through Exit 1; take a right at Busan Bank and walk until you reach a four-way intersection - the book street will be on the left. OR Take Busan Subway Line 1 to Jagalchi Station and take Exit 3; take an immediate right and then go straight.

EXPLORE THE BUSAN TOWER

Get a sweeping view of the entire city from this 350-foot-tall tower. It's a particularly impressive way to take in the city lights at night! The tower is also located in Yongdusan Park, which has several other attractions to see before or after the tower.

💸*Budget:* About $6.75

☞ *Getting There:* Take Busan Subway Line 1 to Nampo Station; the tower is about a five minute walk from Exit 7.

THE BUSAN MODERN HISTORY MUSEUM

This museum is small but it's worth an hour or so to wander its fascinating exhibits documenting the Korean War and Busan's heritage as a port town. Some of it can feel propaganda-ish at times, but that actually just gives you more of a feel for South Korea's recent history. And much of the signage is in English!

✒*Budget:* Free

☞*Getting There:* Take Busan Subway Line 2 to Exit 3 and walk for about ten minutes.

VISIT THE SEA LIFE BUSAN AQUARIUM

While you're in Haeundae, make a stop at the Sea Life Aquarium, which has up to 250 species of aquatic life on display. The underwater tunnel is particularly magical and the aquarium full of sharks is surreal. Oh and I swam inside that aquarium. Yep, with the sharks. When the pandemic slows down, check to see if they start to offer shark dives again...

✒*Budget:* About $25

☞ *Getting There:* Take Busan Subway Line 2 to Haeundae Station and leave via Exit 5; it will be about a five minute walk.

GO HIKING

Koreans are obsessed with hiking, especially in Busan! Busan has some of South Korea's best hiking spots, with a trail for every fitness level.

→ If you're looking for an easy hike, check out Geumnyeongsan Mountain.
→ Moderate hikers will love the trails at Igidae Park.
→ For more advanced trails with absolutely stunning views, challenge yourself to Songaksan Mountain.

VISIT THESE TEMPLES AND PALACES

◊ Seokbulsa Temple

If I had to pick a favorite temple in South Korea, this would be it. There's no other word for it except awe-inspiring. It's out of the way so tends to be less crowded; in fact, you have to hike in to get to the main temple area. You'll be glad you made the effort, though, once you reach the top and see Busan stretching in the distance, framed by Seokbulsa's dramatic, 30-foot high statues carved into the face of the mountain.

Pro Tip: It's super easy to get lost getting to Seokbulsa; in fact, my first visit turned into a six-hour hike. Kakao Maps seems to have pretty good guidance, so make sure you have that downloaded, or check out the basic directions below.

Budget: Free

☞ **Getting There:** There are two ways to get to Seokbulsa. The most straightforward way is to take Busan Subway Line 3 to Mandeok Station; take Exit 2 and follow this road for about an hour (you'll keep left when it forks).

The more interesting but longer journey takes you from Oncheonjang Station (Subway Line 1, Exit 1) to Geumjeong Mountain, where you'll catch the Geumgang Park cable car (around $5); from there, you'll have about a 90-minute hike to the temple, following signs for Namun (South) Gate and going through Namun Village. At the end of the village, you'll turn right and then immediately left to follow the trail down until you meet up with the paved road that leads up to Seokbulsa.

◊ **Geumjeongsanseong Fortress**

If you choose to visit Seokbulsa via the more adventurous route, stop here at Geumjeongsanseong Fortress after you get off the cable car. It's an easy walk from the cable car to the South Gate but if you're up for something more strenuous, spend some time hiking to the North Gate for more exercise and a better view - just bring some water!

Budget: Free

☞ **Getting There:** From Oncheonjang Station (Subway Line 1, Exit 1), head toward Geumjeong Mountain and get on the Geumgang Park cable car (around $5); follow the signs from there to the gate of your choice!

◊ **Samgwangsa Temple**

Known for its stunning pagoda and beautifully painted buildings, Samgwangsa Temple is regularly named one of the most beautiful places to visit in South Korea. Come here especially for the Lantern Festival to celebrate the Buddha's birthday, when thousands of colored lanterns are illuminated at night.

Budget: Free

☞ **Getting There:** Head to the Lotte Department Store in Seomyeon and get on mini bus 15 to Samgwangsa. Alternatively, just hop in a taxi.

◊ Haedong Yonggungsa (The Water Temple)

Haedong Yonggungsa is one of South Korea's only temples overlooking the ocean and also one of only three temples dedicated to the Buddhist Goddess of Mercy, Quan Yin. Combine dramatic panoramic views with a history steeped in mysticism and magic, and you've got the recipe for a truly unique house of worship! Head to Haedong any time but especially for the celebration of the Buddha's birth in the spring, when the temple is decked out in thousands of colorful, lotus-shaped lanterns.

Budget: Free

☞ **Getting There:** Take Busan Subway Line 2 to Haeundae Station; go through Exit 7 and get on Bus 181. You'll get off at the Yonggungsa Temple stop. The bus trip will take about an hour; you can also grab a taxi from Haeundae Station but it will cost you more.

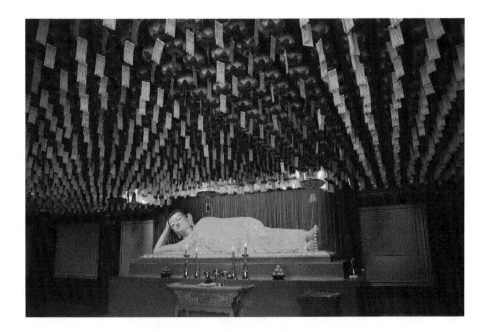

Festivals to Attend in Busan

THE BUSAN FIREWORKS FESTIVAL

South Korea does not kid around when it comes to fireworks shows. The Busan Fireworks Festival, held every year in the autumn, attracts millions of visitors to the city to watch as tens of thousands of fireworks light up the sky over Gwangan Bridge. The festival also features street performances and of course, tons of food and vendors.

The festival has been on pause since COVID but it won't hurt to do a quick Google to see if it has been revived yet!

THE BUSAN INTERNATIONAL FILM FESTIVAL

Held annually in October, the Busan International Film Festival (BIFF) is one of Asia's most important film festivals. Its goal is to introduce new films and first-time directors to the international stage and it features both local and international films. The Open Cinema portion of the festival is particularly popular with its open-air screenings. If you're a movie buff, try not to miss this one!

⊙ **When:** Typically, in Autumn

📍 **Where:** Centum City

🎞️**Budget:** Around $5 for a general screening ticket and $25 to the opening/ closing screening and ceremonies.

Hey. You won't regret taking this trip. In fact, it will change your life for the better. Don't hesitate. Just go.

SHOPPING IN BUSAN

Girl Talk for a Moment...

I can't tell you how many times I had a Korean retail personnel tell me that she doesn't have clothes my size and encourage me not to enter her store. One woman even refused to sell me a dress at the register because she insisted it wouldn't fit me. Listen, I have watched this happen to even the smallest of my girlfriends. It's not you. It's either genuinely-concerned-for-your-wallet Korean culture or...some other version of Korean culture that I don't understand. If this happens to you, just smile and take your money elsewhere.

SHINSEGAE CENTUM CITY

It's easy to lose track of time in the largest shopping complex in the world! From designer clothes and bags to cosmetics and skincare to souvenirs, you'll find everything you could ever need, and plenty of things you never dreamed you wanted, in Shinsegae. If you get tired of shopping, there's also a movie theater, ice rink, and of course - Spa Land.

📍 **Where:** Centum City

☞ **Getting There:** Take Busan Subway Line 2 to the Centum City Station. The station connects directly to the mall so just follow the signs!

GUKJE/NAMPODONG MARKET

You'll already want to come here for street food, but that's not all Gukje Market has to tempt you with. This traditional market is a great place to find bargains on bags and luggage, shoes, home goods, and more. The covered shopping arcade is massive but it's organized (somewhat) into zones to make it a little less overwhelming.

Fun Fact: This market was established by refugees after the Korean War and remains an important cultural area for Busan locals. Don't forget to look up and awe at the architecture.

♀ *Where:* Nampo-dong

☞ *Getting There:* Take Busan Subway Line 1 to Jagalchi Market and take Exit 7. Take the second road on your left.

PNU SHOPPING TOWN AND BEAUTY TOWN

Located in the hip university neighborhood, these shopping areas cater to a younger crowd. The shopping district starts at the main gate of PNU and has a variety of cute boutiques with international and local brands.

Pro Tip: If you pay cash, some places may give you a discount!

♀ *Where:* PNU

☞ *Getting There:* Take Busan Subway Line 1 to the PNU Station. Leave through Exit 3 and go straight.

BUSAN SUBWAY STATIONS

Man, these little stalls inside subway stations always got me when I was coming home from a drunk night out. You'll pass by countless clothing and knick knack stalls in most underground subway stations whether you want to shop or not.

South Korea Notes...

WHERE TO PARTY
IN BUSAN

THURSDAY PARTY

The #1 bar for expats, teachers, and military dudes who want to play beer pong, darts, and foosball while mingling with hotties from around the world. The draft beer is cheap and they give you little bowls of snacks. This place is fun! My only question is WHY do they not have special promotions on Thursdays.... come on, guys!

You are going to find Thursday Parties all over the country! Here are the Thursday Party bars in Busan in ranking of best to still-good-to-drink-at.

◇ Thursday Party Haeundae

◇ Thursday Party Seomyeon

◇Thursday Party Gwangalli

⊙ **Open:** Depends on the location. Pre-pandemic, they were open all day. Now they open around dinner and close before sunrise (4-6am).

WOLFHOUND IRISH PUB

Okay let me be honest. This is the place I'd come to sit at the bar or a table, and order dinner and pre-drink before I'd go to Thursday Party. However, oftentimes, I'd meet some cool people and end up staying at Wolfhound until 1am drinking more. And.... then I'd come back at 10am for hangover breakfasts and drinks (pre-pandemic but let's hope they change their hours soon).

⊙ **Open:** 6pm-1am M-F; 12pm-1am weekends

♀ **Where:** Haeundae

🏠**Address:** 13 Haeundaehaebyeon-ro 265beon-gi

THE VINYL UNDERGROUND

One of Busan's longest running live music venues, The Vinyl Underground has a big dance floor and features a range of genres, from hip-hop to rock and roll. It's in the PNU area and close to Gwangali so the crowd is young and energetic! Whether you're coming for a long night or just want to dip your toes in for a couple drinks, this place never fails to entertain.

○ **Open:** 8pm-2am; closed Sunday and Monday

♥ **Where:** PNU

📇 **Address:** 58-2 Daeyeon-dong, Nam-gu Busan

HQ GWANGALI

This beachfront expat hotspot has a great view and a great, reasonably priced drink menu. In addition to its frequent live music, the bar also runs fun weekly trivia nights! Not to mention, I could eat their chicken wings every night of the week!

Check out their Facebook page (Hq Bar) to see their schedule.

○ **Open:** The weirdest hours, please check their Facebook, I can't keep up.

♥ **Where:** The entrance is directly on Gwangalli beach inside a tall building. There is a well-known "Burger and Pasta" on the first floor. Go in the building and take the elevator to the 4th floor.

📇 **Address:** 179-21 Millak-dong, Suyeong-gu, Busan

𝐟 hq.bar.5

BILLIE JEAN

Not a bar but not yet a nightclub. Dance the night away at this western-style club in Haeundae's Dalmaji Hill area. The music ranges from rock and roll to funk and hip-hop, and the bartenders get involved with fun cocktail shows. Dress cute but be prepared to get a little sweaty.

○ **Open:** Sun-Thurs 7pm-3am; Fri-Sat 7pm-4am

♥ **Where:** Haeundae

📇 **Address:** 22 Dalmaji-gil, Haeundae-gu Busan

CLUB MONK

Enjoy a low-key crowd, classic jazz, and a silky glass of wine at Club MONK. There's live jazz from 9pm-11pm every night except Sunday, and they often host other types of artists and events as well. Follow their Facebook page for their schedule.

○ **Open:** 6:30pm-2am

♥ **Where:** Gwangali

📇 **Address:** 58-34 Daeyeon 3(sam)-dong, Nam-gu Busan

𝐟 JazzClubMonk

Nightclubs

OUTPUT BUSAN

If EDM is more your style, head over to Output Busan in Seomyeon. This club has an industrial-chic vibe and hosts some of Busan's best underground DJs. I didn't even know that I liked this kind of music until I came here...give it a shot. Plus, you get to mingle with some of the coolest Koreans I've ever seen.

⊙ *Open:* Thurs-Sat 9pm-5am

♥ *Where:* Seomyeon

🚉*Address:* 36 Seojeon-ro 10beon-gil, Busan

f OUTPUTBUSAN

REVEL CLUB

This huge venue is probably Busan's best-known club. It caters to the hip-hop crowd and has two dance floors that feature both local and international DJs. It fits up to 1,000 people and since it's located in the university area, the crowd is young, lively, and fun! Cover charge is around $9.

⊙ *Open:* Sat-Sun 10pm-5am

♥ *Where:* PNU

🚉*Address:* 3 Yongso-ro 28beon-gil, Nam-gu Busan

f REVEL051

Hey...

HAVE YOU TUNED IN YET?

THIS IS MY FAVORITE TRAVEL PLAYLIST EVER!

BEST SPAS
IN BUSAN

(For the hangovers)

These spas and jjimjilbangs are all similar yet different in their own ways, so let me give you a quick top 3 list of my favorite spas in Busan.

01

Hurshimchung with
Hot Springs,
Dongnae District

02

Spa Land at Shinsegae,
Centum City

03

Haeundae Spa Center,
Haeundae

(you can sleep here!)

Hey...

Still nervous to travel alone? That's okay. I still get nervous before I go to a new city or country. The feeling doesn't go away. But my attitude towards my nervousness has evolved. Instead of treating these nerves as anxiety and fear, I treat them as excitement and anticipation. A "I just want to get there already" feeling. Nerves mean that you're alive. Embrace them and live life outside your comfort zone. Be proud of your nerves...some people live without them.

CHAPTER THREE

—

Gangneung

—

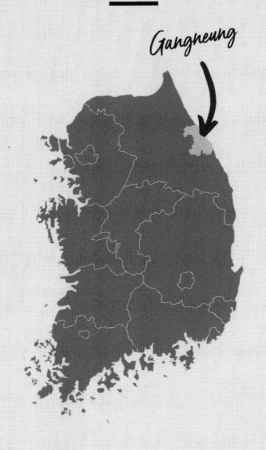

Gangneung

INTRODUCTION
TO GANGNEUNG

Tired of being surrounded by expats? Get a little more off-the-beaten-track in Gangneung! This charming city nestled along South Korea's northeast coast combines stunningly preserved historical and cultural treasures with funky modern fun. Add in beautiful beaches and a thriving local coffee scene, and you've got a great place to spend a few days!

Start your day with a buzz on Anmok Coffee Street. Step back in time with a stroll through traditional buildings dating back to the 1500s. Sample tofu so silky and luscious, it'll satisfy even the pickiest carnivores. Take a leisurely bike ride around Gyeongpo Lake or challenge your fear of heights on Jeongdongjin's glass-bottomed bridge. Overwhelm your senses with a walk through Jungang Market, one of South Korea's most authentic traditional markets.

Between its picturesque scenery, its mouth-watering local delicacies, and it's warm, welcoming people, Gangneung will capture your heart for sure!

Getting there from Seoul

Gangneung is just a hop, skip, and a jump from Seoul so it's quick and easy to add it to your itinerary!

By Train

The KTX train is really the only way I recommend traveling from Seoul to Gangneung. It's cheap, simple, and comfortable, so it's really a no-brainer!

⊘ **When:** The trip from Seoul to Gangneung will take about two hours. Trains run from around 9am to around 5pm depending on the date.

📍 **Where:** Get on the KTX at Seoul Station; you can buy your tickets there at the Korail Office, or you can buy them in advance online ☞

💸 **How Much:** $17-25 depending on whether you ride at peak or non-peak hours.

By Bus

You can also get to Gangneung by bus, although this will take longer than by train. There are two bus stations in Gangneung: the newer one, which is further from the city center, and the older station, which is closer to the city.

⊘ **When:** The bus trip will take about three hours. Buses from every 30-15 minutes from 6:30am-11pm.

📍 **Where:** Buy your ticket and get on at the Dong Seoul Bus Terminal (Seoul Subway Line 2, Exit 4) or the Seoul Express Bus Terminal in Gangnam (Seoul Subway Line 3, Exit 1).

💸 **How Much:** $11-17

Getting around Gangneung

Gangneung is fairly spread out so unless you plan to stay in just one area, walking isn't really a good way to get around. Instead, use a combination of these options!

By Bus

Gangneung's local bus system will take you pretty much anywhere you want to go. Unfortunately, there's few English signs so it can be a little confusing if you don't read Korean.

💵 **How Much:** $.50-$2.00 depending on where you're going - make sure to bring small bills!

Pro Tip: Make sure you have Naver Maps downloaded, and write down the name of your stop in hangul. It's also helpful to know how to say your stop in Korean so that you can tell the bus driver where to let you off!

By Taxi/Car

Yes, it will cost you a bit more, but taking taxis or renting a car will save you the hassle and confusion of figuring out the local bus schedule.

◊**Taxi:** You can grab a taxi at the bus or train station and at major tourist destinations (like the beaches). Your hotel staff can also call you a cab, and many restaurants are also willing to do so!

💵 **How Much:** $5-20 depending on where you're going.

◊ **Car:** If you have your international driver's license, renting a car is a super easy option! You won't be constrained by bus schedules or worry about flagging down a cab. There are multiple car rental agencies in Gangneung and nearby Jeongdongjin.

💵 **How Much:** About $50 a day

By Bike

There are a ton of bike rental places, particularly near the beaches and the lake. While I wouldn't plan to use a bike exclusively for your entire time there, it's a good way to explore the boardwalk and beach areas!

Pro Tip: When in doubt, ask the staff at your hotel the best way to get where you want to go. They'll be able to give you specific bus instructions or call you a cab and give the driver directions - and it's not unheard of for hotel staff to just offer to drive you themselves!

NEIGHBORHOODS IN GANGNEUNG

Unlike Seoul and Busan, Gangneung doesn't have a ton of individual neighborhoods. You'll basically split your time between the city center and the beach areas.

GYO-DONG

One of Gangneung's most walkable areas, Gyo-dong is in the heart of the city. Think shopping, nightlife, and street food!

SONGJEONG-DONG, GYEONSO-DONG, AND ANHYEON-DONG

Gangneung has several can't-miss beaches scattered throughout these three coastal neighborhoods. You'll also want to hit Gyeongso-dong to visit the city's coffee hub, Anmok Coffee Street!

GYEONGPO-DONG

Gyeongpo-dong technically overlaps with some of the beach neighborhoods so it's easy to kill two birds with one stone. Come here for some of Gangneung's most beautiful vistas, including Gyeongpodae Lake.

JEONGDONGJIN

Jeongdongjin is a bit of a trek outside the center of Gangneung but it's worth a visit! It's got its own beautiful beach, which is watched over by the iconic Sun Cruise Hotel - literally a giant cruise ship on top of the bluffs over the ocean. Enjoy delicious seafood and several quirky museums. Early risers won't want to miss sunrise at Sculpture Park!

Fun Fact!

For three weeks after a baby is born, the family hangs a straw rope of chili peppers or pine needles across the door of the house to frighten away evil spirits.

WHERE TO STAY IN GANGNEUNG

GANGNEUNG HERREN HAUS

Beachfront with ocean views from your impeccably clean room! Come and unwind on Herren Haus's trendy rooftop patio and take in the gorgeous water views. There's a cute little cafe on the first floor and you're just steps from the water!

Budget: $$$

☆ *Style:* Private rooms

♥ *Where:* Beachside

Address: 16, Changhae-ro 14beon-gil, 210-150 Gangneung

 BOOK HERE

HOTEL EAST9

Modern rooms, glittering city views, and central yet quiet location make this hotel a great choice for exploring Gangneung! You'll be in a super walkable area, close to a ton of dining options, shopping, and sightseeing. There's a decent continental breakfast, and the 24-hour front desk staff is always happy to help with recommendations.

Budget: $$

☆ *Style:* Private rooms

♥ *Where:* City center

Address: 8-6, Gyodonggwangjang-ro 100beon-gil, 25512 Gangneung

BOOK HERE

BOUTIQUE HOTEL BOMBOM

You'll get style, convenience, and luxury with this hotel pick! From the floor-to-ceiling windows and walk-in rain shower to the delicious on-site restaurant, everything has been arranged flawlessly for a breezy, comfortable stay. You can walk anywhere and everywhere your heart desires and the front desk concierge is happy to point you in the right direction.

💵 *Budget:* $$

☆ *Style:* Private rooms

📍 *Where:* Outer edge of the city

🏨 *Address:* 1871-4, Kyo-dong, 25512 Gangneung

BOOK HERE

DAL GARAM GUESTHOUSE

When you're new to a city, there is nothing more valuable than a host that is eager to help you navigate. You are not alone when you stay at Dal Garam Guesthouse. They've thought of every details from

The cozy lounge area to the perfect breakfast. Staying here means that you're in a fabulous location to explore the city on foot.

💵 *Budget:* $$

☆ *Style:* Private Rooms

📍 *Where:* Central

🏨 *Address:* 9, Sumun-gil 19beon-gil, 25555 Gangneung

BOOK HERE

GANGNEUNG GUESTHOUSE MYU

You'll be just a short walk from some of Gangneung's best street food at this guesthouse! Its central city location also puts you close to sightseeing and transportation. The staff are incredibly friendly and helpful, and the guest house is perfectly laid out to make some new friends for exploring. This is an easy, safe choice if you're on a budget.

💸 **Budget:** $

☆ **Style:** Dorms

📍 **Where:** City center

🏛 **Address:** 3Floor, 2068-1, Gyeonggang-ro, Gangneung-si

 BOOK HERE

AARK HOUSE

This adorable hostel has it all — location, charm, and a killer breakfast! Just 5 minutes from the main train station and 10 from the bus station, it's easy to get to anywhere in the city. You can even take casual Korean lessons from the amazingly friendly hosts!

💸 **Budget:** $

☆ **Style:** Dorm-style

📍 **Where:** Right by the river

🏛 **Address:** 4-5, Yongji-ro 96beon-gil

 BOOK HERE

Fun Fact!

Toilet paper and tissues are common housewarming gifts.

WHERE TO EAT
IN GANGNEUNG

Coffee Shops

BOHEMIAN COFFEE

There are a couple branches of this family-owned roastery in Gangneung, but this one is convenient to the city center. The baristas specialize in hand-drip coffee, which can sometimes be hard to find in South Korea, and the espressos are strong and rich. You can get brunch here as well on the first floor - try the potato croquettes!

⊙ **Open:** 8am-10pm

📍 **Where:** Gyo-dong

🏫 **Address:** 482-1 Gyo-dong, Gangneung-si, Gangwon-do

UNCLE BOB

The coffee here is excellent, the food is well made, and the atmosphere is adorable, but the real draw is the foreign owner. "Uncle" Bob is chatty and knowledgeable about everything from coffee and Korean culture, and he's happy to sit and talk with you. The cafe is also dog-friendly!

⊙ **Open:** 8:30am-10pm

📍 **Where:** Ponam-dong

🏫 **Address:** 81-5 Nanseolheon-ro, Ponam 2(i)-dong, Gangneung-si, Gangwon-do

GANGNEUNG COFFEE STREET

Literally any shop on this famous street is a great place to get your caffeine fix! Of course, you'll see the inescapable Starbucks but there are dozens of other mom-and-pop places to sample the local roasters and homemade sweets. Just follow your nose and you can't go wrong!

⊙ **Open:** 8:30am-10pm

📍 **Where:** Gyeongso-dong

🏫 **Address:** 17, Changhae-ro, Gangneung-si, Gangwon-do

Breakfast & Brunch

You can grab a decent (if not delicious!) breakfast at virtually any of Gangneung's coffee shops, but here are a few more options to get you started for the day.

CAFE HASSOME GANGNEUNG

This cafe is close to the beach and has spacious table and bar seating, making it a great place to grab coffee and brunch with friends before hitting the sand for the day. You can't miss it thanks to the giant Coca-Cola pandas draped over the top of the building!

⊙ **Open:** 11am-10pm

♥ **Where:** Chodang-dong (near Songjeong-dong)

🏛**Address:** 14 Gangneung-daero 587beon-gil, Chodang-dong, Gangneung-si, Gangwon-do

DONGHWA GARDEN

These spicy stews will warm up even the coldest winter morning! They've got delicious seafood and vegetarian options, as well as a particularly pungent bean paste stew. This place gets packed so even though it's open all day, it's best to come here first thing in the morning before they run out!

⊙ **Open:** 7am-7pm; break time from 4-5pm

♥ **Where:** Chodang-dong

🏛**Address:** 309-1, Chodang-dong, Gangneung-si, Gangwon-do

Lunch

ALIVE HOME

This Japanese homestyle restaurant serves up killer Japanese curry, potato croquettes, rice bowls, and ice cold beer. It's small so there's usually a wait, but the staff are friendly and everything moves quickly.

⊙ **Open:** 11:30am-3pm; 5pm-8pm

♥ **Where:** Gyo-dong

GU-ICHON

Gu-Ichon is known for its rich pork belly dishes. Pair it with a bowl of miso bibimbap and you'll be full for hours for a very reasonable price!

⊙ **Open:** 11:30am-11pm; closed Sundays

♥ **Where:** Gyo-dong

🏛**Address:** 1833-7 Gyo 1(il)-dong, Gangneung-si, Gangwon-do

PONAM SAGOL ONGSIMI

Locals swear by this restaurant for traditional ongsimi, potato dumpling soup that's the ultimate comfort food. The dumplings are pillowy and the creamy beef broth compliments them perfectly. Service is focused on efficiency - don't expect a lot of small talk!

☉ *Open:* 11:30am-2:30pm; 3:30pm-7:30pm M-W; 11:30am-3pm; 4pm-7:30pm Sat-Sun

♥ *Where:* Ponam-dong (outside of Gyo-dong)

🚏*Address:* 11 Namgu-gil 10beon-gil, Ponam 1(il)-dong, Gangneung-si, Gangwon-do

SONGPO SEAFOOD & SASHIMI

A beachfront sashimi restaurant open 24 hours? Music to my ears! They've got an English menu (always a plus!), and of course the gorgeous water views. If raw fish isn't your thing, you should still come here for the grilled mackerel.

☉ *Open:* 24 hours a day, baby!

♥ *Where:* Anhyeon-dong (right on Gyeongpo Beach)

🚏*Address:* 451, Changhae-Ro, Gangneung, Gangwon-do

Dinner

HANAM PIG HOUSE GANGNUENG IBAM

Craving Korean BBQ? Don't miss this outstanding pork BBQ restaurant just outside of the city center. The staff is incredibly friendly and will make sure your dinner is cooked to absolute perfection. It's also open late so it's a good place to stop after a night out.

☉ *Open:* 5pm-midnight

♥ *Where:* Ibam-dong (near Gyo-dong)

🚏*Address:*286 Ibam-dong, Gangneung-si, Gangwon-do

HAPPINESS DUMPLINGS GIMBAP

The name says it all - this place serves up true joy in perfect little dough pillows! Try the curry dumplings and the kimchi dumplings. You can fill up for cheap, too - one order comes with 10 pieces!

☉ *Open:* 8am-10pm

♥ *Where:* Ibam-dong (outside of Gyo-dong)

🚏*Address:* 153, Ipam-Ro, Gangneung, Gangwon-do

RUI KITCHEN

This Japanese-western fusion restaurant is a favorite on Gyeongpo Beach. Rich pork and cheese cutlets, steaming bowls of rice, and salty miso soup - it doesn't get any better!

☉ **Open:** 11am-9:30pm; closed Mondays

♀ **Where:** Anhyeon-dong

🏯 **Address:** 439, Changhae-ro 1F, Gangneung, Gangwon-do

Street Food

CHODANG DUBU (TOFU) VILLAGE

Oh, sundubu-jjigae . . . hearty bowls of spicy broth with fresh-cracked egg and melt-in-your-mouth tofu. This life-altering dish is made even more special in Chodang Tofu Village. The tofu from this area of South Korea is made with seaweed-infused water, giving it a distinctive flavor and extra creamy texture.

Don't just stop at the sundubu-jjigae, though. The Village features dozens of tofu-centric restaurants serving up their own specialties, including porridge and curry dishes.

♀ **Where:** Chodang-dong

🏯 **Address:** 47 Chodangsundubu-gil, Gangmun-dong, Gangneung-si, Gangwon-do

Pro Tip: Many restaurants in the Village are open for lunch but not dinner. If you're planning a food crawl, plan to start around 11 so you don't miss out!

JUNGANG MARKET

This uber-traditional Korean market is filled with street food stalls ranging from the sweet to the spicy to the truly outlandish (think silkworm larvae)!

♀ **Where:** Gyo-dong

🏯 **Address:** 21 Geumseong-ro, Jungang-dong, Gangneung-si, Gangwon-do

GANGNEUNG CENTRAL MARKET

End a day of beach-hopping with a street food dinner at Gangneung Central Market. Start with some sweet and spicy fried chicken or fresh king crab. For dessert, try the hotteok (sweet pancake) filled with ice cream or cheese, or if you're feeling more adventurous, stop by Masiwa for some squid ice cream.

♀ **Where:** Songjeong-dong (near Anmok Beach)

🏯 **Address:** 2398-10 Gyeonggang-ro, Songjeong-dong, Gangneung-si, Gangwon-do

WHERE TO DRINK IN GANGNEUNG

BUDNAMU BREWERY

The heart of Gangneung's craft brewing scene, Budnamu is beloved for its creative local beers and fun staff. It's got a unique industrial atmosphere and excellent bar food - the kimchi pizza and mac-and-cheese are always a hit!

⊙ **Open:** 10am-1am

♥ **Where:** Gyo-dong

🏛**Address:** 1961 Gyunggangro | 93-8 Hongje-dong, Gangneung, Gangwon-do

WAREHOUSE

If you're looking for a place to party, look no further than Warehouse! Located in the heart of Gangneung's downtown, this place is known for its laidback crowd and casual vibe. You can play pool, darts, and even beer pong, and there's live music on the weekends. They don't serve food but you're welcome to bring in your own!

⊙ **Open:** 10am-1am 8pm-4am Sun-Thurs; 8pm-5am Fri-Sat

♥ **Where:** Gyo-dong

🏛**Address:** 9-1 Seongnae-dong Gangneung, Gangwon-do

RUSH

Owned by two musician brothers, Rush prides itself on excellent local music and true Gangneung hospitality. Acts vary from rock to hip-hop to blues, and the atmosphere is delightfully divey!

⊙ **Open:** 10am-1am7:30pm-4am (or later, depending on the crowd and the show!

♥ **Where:** Gyo-dong

🏛**Address:** 번지 지하 1829-4, Gyo-dong, Gangneung-si, Gangwon-do

SHOPPING IN GANGNEUNG

JUNGANG MARKET

Come here for the street food, yes, but also the shopping! This traditional market is divided into two main sections: a traditional market with vendors splayed out on the streets and an underground fish market. There are also restaurants and cafes, plus a decent hanbok shop, on the second floor of the arcade.

♀ Where: Gyo-dong

🏛Address: 21 Geumseong-ro, Jungang-dong, Gangneung-si, Gangwon-do

GANGNEUNG CENTRAL MARKET

Another traditional local market, Gangneung Central Market is a covered arcade filled with street food, cosmetics, clothes, and more.

♀ Where: Songjeong-dong (near Anmok Beach)

🏛Address: 2398-10 Gyeonggang-ro, Songjeong-dong, Gangneung-si, Gangwon-do

Pro Tip: Give Koreans sincere compliments when you feel them. They aren't used to hearing them from strangers…especially foreigners. A simple, "you have beautiful eyes", or "I love your dress" will go a long way and make someone's day.

THINGS TO DO
IN GANGNEUNG

HIT THE BEACHES

South Korea is loaded with beaches, and Gangneung has some of the east coast's best. They're quieter than the party beaches of Busan but still packed with picturesque views, mouth-watering seafood, and ice cold beer.

You can't go wrong visiting any of the area's 20+ beaches, but here are some of the most popular.

◊ **Gyeongpo Beach:** Often named as the most beautiful beach on South Korea's east coast, Gyeongpo is hugely popular with locals and tourists alike. It's technically a sandbar between the ocean and Gyeongpo Lake, so you have water views on both sides. Into water sports? You can go tubing or paragliding and rent jet skis and boats. There's a great sauna at the St. John's Hotel nearby, as well as a ton of restaurants and cafes.

◊ **Jeongdongjin Beach:** A scenic train ride away from Gangneung city center, this serene beach glistens with sea glass. It's the perfect spot to relax with a book and a beer, and it's also got some killer seafood restaurants.

◊ **Anmok Beach:** White sand, blue water, mountain views, and black coffee - what more does a girl need? Anmok gets packed during the summer months, so it's a cool place to experience the real South Korean beach culture! You can also rent umbrellas and boats during the summer.

◊ **Gangmun Beach:** This gigantic beach on the East Sea is known for its cold water and big waves. Thanks to its space, it's generally pretty quiet. It's a great place to watch the sunset, and there are some swanky hotels nearby where you can grab a cocktail or dinner.

CYCLE AROUND GYEONGPO LAKE

Gyeongpo Lake offers more than just beautiful beach views! You can walk or cycle on a miles-long path through wetlands and gardens. The statutes dotting the park tell the story of South Korea's version of Robin Hood, and the Gyeongpodae Pavilion offers a stunning view of the water. It's also famous for its stunning full moon views!

EXPERIENCE A KOREAN FESTIVAL

South Koreans love a party! There are virtually countless local and national festivals sprinkled throughout the year, and Gangneung has some truly unique ones. Catch the Cherry Blossom Festival at Gyeongpo Lake in the spring (the exact dates vary depending on when the flowers bloom) or the Gangneung Coffee Festival, typically held in the fall. Not to be missed is the Danoje Festival in June, celebrating traditional Korean shaman culture. You can watch traditional wrestling and other cultural performances, wash your hair in iris water for renewal and purification, and of course eat and drink to your heart's content! Danoje turns into quite a party at night as well, complete with fireworks shows and soju galore.

TRY THE LOCAL DELICACIES

In addition to the coffee, Gangneung is famous for its own take on several traditional dishes. Try abalone juk (rice porridge), seop-guk (mussel stew), gamjajeon (potato pancakes), dakgangjeong (fried chicken), and of course, sundubu-jjigae (spicy tofu and seafood stew).

WATCH THE SUNRISE AT SCULPTURE PARK

The sculpture park at the Sea Cruise Hotel in Jeongdongjin is one of the best places in the entire country to catch a glorious sunrise. The park grounds look out over the ocean, giving you a completely unobstructed view. If you really want to step into the horizon, take a walk over the glass-bottomed bridge!

🏷️ **Budget:** $5 entrance fee

South Korea Notes...

....

....

....

....

You and me. We are special.
How many girls do you know in your hometown that
would make a move this bold?
You're a bad bitch. And I like that about you.

Sightseeing in Gangneung

OJUKHEON HOUSE

This famous residential complex was built in the 1500s for Yulgok Yi Yi, a famous scholar, and his mother, an equally famous artist (fun fact: their faces grace the 5,000 won and 50,000 won notes!). The buildings have been impeccably preserved, and the museum houses loads of interesting artifacts, art, and calligraphy from the era.

♥ **Where:** Gyeongpo-dong

☉ **Open:** 9am-5pm

✐ **Budget:** $2.50

SEONGYOJANG HOUSE

Need more of a history fix? Stop by Seongyojang House! One of South Korea's National Important Cultural Properties, this 300-year-old complex has almost 100 traditional rooms you can explore. It historically housed poets and artists, and some of the original poetry written here is framed on the walls. The complex has been made even more famous by its appearance in a ton of Korean movies and dramas!

♥ **Where:** Gyeonpo-dong

☉ **Open:** 9am-6pm

✐ **Budget:** $3

Pro Tip: Buy some of the local gochujang (red chili paste) or doenjang (soybean paste)!

CHARMSORI GRAMOPHONE & EDISON SCIENCE MUSEUM

What? Gramophones and lightbulbs don't sound exciting to you? Hear me out here - this quirky museum is totally worth your time! It was started by a local collector who spent over five decades traveling the world and amassing this huge collection of Edison's inventions. Many of the pieces still work, and listening to music played on an original Edison gramophone is a truly unique experience!

♥ Where: Gyeongpo-dong

☉ Open: 9am-6pm

✈ Budget: $10

SANDGLASS (HOURGLASS) PARK

Built in 1999 to commemorate the new century, Sandglass Park in Jeong-dongjin is home to the world's largest working hourglass. It holds 8 tons of sand and takes an entire year for the sand to trickle from the top of the glass to the bottom; it resets every year at midnight on New Year's Day. The park is accessible from Jeongdongjin Beach and you can also visit the Jeongdongjin Time Museum, located inside a steam train.

♥ Where: Jeongdongjin

☉ Open: 9am-6pm

✈ Budget: $5

HASLLA ART WORLD

Another charmingly Korean museum, Haslla Art World consists of 61 acres of unique exhibits. There's a modern art section, an outdoor sculpture section, and a quirky (or creepy, depending on your personal opinion!) Pinocchio section featuring hordes of creative marionettes.

♥ Where: Jeongdongjin

☉ Open: 8:30am-6:30pm

✈ Budget: $8

—

CHAPTER FOUR

Gyeongju

—

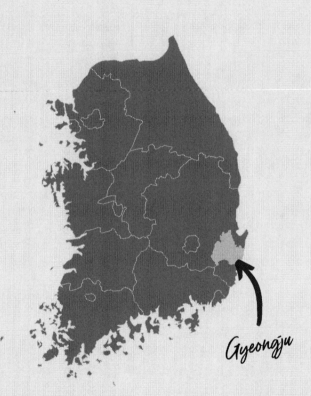

Gyeongju

INTRODUCTION
TO GYEONGJU

Step back in time in Gyeongju, South Korea's ancient capital, where the splendor and mystery of the fabled Silla Kingdom will greet you around every turn.

Gyeonju was home to the rich and famous of the Silla elite, and it's known as "the museum without walls" for good reason! This city has more palatial ruins, Buddhist art, temples, lavish tombs, and other historical artifacts than any other single place in South Korea. It's virtually impossible to run out of things to see in this UNESCO World Heritage Site.

Wander through traditional villages and tomb complexes dedicated to nobles and kings. Visit the oldest surviving astronomical observatory in Asia. Spend a night in one of the most gorgeous Buddhist temples in South Korea. Stroll through astounding tumuli, gigantic ancient burial mounds that dominate the city's landscape. Gorge on ssambap, lettuce wraps stuffed with every Korean goodie imaginable, and wash it down with beopju, a locally made sweet rice wine whose recipe has been passed down for generations.

Gyeongju is a far cry from the high-tech intensity of Seoul and Busan, so if you're looking for a break from the bright lights and the 24-hour party, you've found it!

Getting to Gyeongju

Gyeongju is well connected to South Korea's other major cities by public transport so reaching the city is pretty seamless!

By Train

The fastest way to get to Gyeongju is by train. There are a few train options to choose from (express, slower commuter train, and combination of the two), but these are my top picks for the most convenient!

◊**From Seoul:** Hop on the KTX at Seoul Station and take the high-speed train to Dongdaegu Station; from there, transfer to the regular commuter train to Gyeongju Station, which is in the center of the city. (You can also take the KTX all the way to Singyeongju Station without transferring, but then you'll need to take a bus into the city).

⊙ **When:** KTX trains run from 9:30am - 9:30pm, every 30-90 minutes. Local trains from Dongdaegu run approximately every 20 minutes. The trip will take about 3 hours total.

♥ **Where:** Look for the KoRail / KTX office in Seoul Station.

💸 **How Much:** About $36-40

◊**From Busan:** Get on the SRT fast train at Busan Station and take it to Singyeongju Station; from there, transfer to Bus 70 to Gyeongju Station.

⊙ **When:** SRT trains leave from Busan about once an hour from 6:50am-10pm. Bus 70 runs from Singyeongju to Gyeongju every 10 minutes or so until 9pm. The trip will take about 90 minutes.

♥ **Where:** Look for the SRT / KoRail office or touch-screen vending machines in Busan Station.

💸 **How Much:** $12-15

Getting around Gyeongju

Gyeongju doesn't have a subway system but the city's buses and taxis will take you anywhere you want to go. For even more freedom of movement, consider renting a car.

By Bus

Good news - buses are actually pretty straightforward in Gyeongju! You can use Bus 10 (clockwise route around the city) and Bus 11 (counterclockwise route) to hit up most of the major tourist spots. These buses also stop at the city's bus terminals and train station.

The buses have recorded messages in English announcing the next stop, eliminating the need to try to learn the name of your stop in Korean. And they're extremely budget-friendly, running you about $1.25 per ride.

By Taxi

Don't want to be tied down by a bus schedule (or deal with packed buses on the weekends)? Flag a taxi at any major tourist destination, bus station, or train station. Many taxis are also available for hire for a full day, which can take a lot of the guesswork out of your itinerary.

Short rides will cost anywhere from $3-10. You can get a day rental (5-8 hours) for around $125-175.

By Car

If you've got your international driver's license on stand-by, Gyeongju is the perfect spot to use it. There are a couple of rental car options near the train station, and you can usually also ask your hotel reception staff for help renting a vehicle. You can often find rental car deals starting at around $60 a day.

By Bike

You probably don't want to go with this option during the height of the winter cold or summer humidity, but if the weather is nice, biking is a great way to take in the beauty of Gyeongju! There are a ton of bike rental places in the city and you can get a set of wheels for about $4 per hour or $20 per day.

NEIGHBORHOODS IN GYEONGJU

Gyeongju is a unique city, filled with dozens of important cultural and historical sites. Surrounded by Gyeongju National Park, the city can be divided into seven main tourist zones - venture to any one of them and you'll find plenty to fill your days!

DOWNTOWN ZONE

As the name suggests, this zone is Gyeongju's modern city center. You'll find many of the city's hotels here, as well as several major tourist attractions, including temples and the Gyeongju National Park sites.

BOMUN TOURIST COMPLEX

Unwind at Gyeongju's serene man-made Bomun Lake, grab a cocktail at one of the nearby posh hotels, or visit one of the city's quirky theme parks.

BULGUKSA ZONE

Two of Gyeongju's most famous temples can be found in this area of the city. You'll also want to stop by the Gyeongju Folk Craft Village to pick up one-of-a-kind local souvenirs!

NAMSAN ZONE

Come here for hiking and (even more) history! Locals often claim that the ancient Silla Kingdom begins and ends in Namsan - it's home to the well where the Kingdom's founder was born, as well as to lavish pavilions where royals feasted in the Kingdom's end days.

DONGHAE ZONE

The easternmost area of Gyeongju, the Donghae Zone stretches to the East Sea and includes a pretty beach and walking trails, as well as another of the city's most famous temples. And of course, seafood!

SEOAK ZONE

This will be your first stop in Gyeongju, since it contains the bus and train stations. But there's a ton else to see here, including ancient tombs and stunning views.

BUKBU ZONE

This zone was the birthplace of Cheondoism, a native Korean religion, and is home to several important Buddhist sites as well. You can also experience what it was like to live in ancient Silla at one of several traditional villages.

WHERE TO STAY IN GYEONGJU

HILTON GYEONGJU

Luxury is the name of the game here at the Hilton! Dine at one of six on-site restaurants and lounge at the indoor and seasonal outdoor pools. Fitness buffs can hit the gym, play a game of squash, or bike around the lake. A bit outside of the city center, the Hilton makes a great place to rest, relax, and enjoy Gyeongju's natural beauty.

Budget: $$$
☆ *Style:* Private rooms
♥ *Where:* Bomun Tourist Complex, on the shores of Bomun Lake
Address: 484-7, Bomun-ro, 38117 Gyeongju

BOOK HERE

DOOBAKI HOSTEL

The social hostel in Gyeongju. Come, meet some other travelers, drink, explore or just chill. The English-speaking owners of this popular hostel will make you feel right at home, and the location in one of the city's central neighborhoods can't be beat. You'll be just minutes from the train and bus stations and close to sightseeing and restaurants.

💸 *Budget:* $

☆ *Style:* Dorms and Private Rooms

📍 *Where:* City center (Dongbu-dong)

🏠 *Address:* 76, Hwarang-ro, 780-060 Gyeongju

 BOOK HERE

G HOUSE MINI HOTEL AND GUESTHOUSE

Perfect for the minimalist, modern solo traveler who wants some alone time! Go for the Korean-style room and experience how Koreans often travel. This mini hotel is near the bus and train stations and is walkable to some of Gyeongju's most famous attractions. Breakfast is included in the price, and the common area has a cool industrial vibe. If you've been traveling for a while, the free laundry facilities are a nice bonus!

💸 *Budget:* $

☆ *Style:* Private Rooms

📍 *Where:* Steps from the major transportation terminals (Noseo-dong)

🏠 *Address:* 10, Wonhyo-ro 26beon-gil, 38157 Gyeongju

 BOOK HERE

GOLGULSA TEMPLE

Martial arts, meditation, and monks - get ready for a once-in-a-lifetime experience! Beautiful Golgulsa Temple has one of the most affordable and unique temple stay programs in all of South Korea. The temple is a Sunmudo (martial arts) training center and visitors get to partake in lessons in the ancient practice, as well as morning and evening meditations and traditional vegetarian Buddhist meals.

🏷 **Budget:** $$

☆ **Style:** Dorm and private rooms (separated by gender)

📍 **Where:** City outskirts, at the foot of Mt. Hamwol

🏛 **Address:** 101-5, Girim-ro, Yangbuk-myeon, Gyeongju-si, Gyeongsangbuk-do

South Korea Notes...

....
....
....
....
....
....
....

KOREANS ARE SOME OF THE LOVELIEST PEOPLE IN THE WORLD. YOUR NEW KOREAN FRIENDS ARE WAITING FOR YOU... YOU JUST HAVEN'T MET THEM YET!

WHERE TO EAT IN GYEONGJU

Coffee Shops

in a convenient central location. The only downside is that, true to South Korean form, they don't open until later!

HWANGNAM BBANG BAKERY

Try your first taste of Hwangnam bread here - it's often touted as the original Hwangnam bakery! The crusty bread is sweet but not overly sweet, and they don't skimp on the red bean paste. You can get a piece of the local delicacy for about a dollar and still have plenty left over for an espresso or one of their other great sweets.

🕐 *Open:* 8am-11pm
📍 *Where:* Downtown Zone
🏛 *Address:* 47-1 Hwango-dong, Gyeongju, Gyeongsangbuk-do

FETE COFFEE

This cafe has a cool atmosphere, friendly staff, and a great flat white. They also serve good food and are

🕐 *Open:* 12pm-9pm
📍 *Where:* Downtown Zone
🏛 *Address:* 1097 Poseok-ro, Hwangnam-dong, Gyeongju-si, Gyeongsangbuk-do

CAFE SABAHA

This spacious cafe designed in traditional Silla style has two floors as well as outdoor seating overlooking the Woljeonggyo Bridge. The interior is casual but elegant and the service is excellent. Their matcha drinks are to die for, and they also serve beer and a small food menu.

🕐 *Open:* 11am-9pm
📍 *Where:* Downtown Zone
🏛 *Address:* 21, Gyochonan-gil, Gyeongju, Gyeongsangbuk-do

CAFE OHI

Come to this rooftop cafe for its homey decor and delicious sweets. They serve coffee and tea, as well as beer and wine, and are open late so you can watch the sunset.

🕐 **Open:** 11am-10pm Wed-Mon; 11am-6pm Tuesdays

📍 **Where:** Downtown Zone

🏛 **Address:** 1070 Poseok-ro, Hwangnam-dong, Gyeongju-si, Gyeongsangbuk-do

Breakfast & Brunch

VENZAMAS

It's a little pricey, but you can get a pretty good western-style brunch at this chic cafe. The place is huge, with four separate buildings, so you rarely have to worry about finding a seat.

🕐 **Open:** 10am-10pm

📍 **Where:** Eastern edge of the Downtown Zone

🏛 **Address:** 2 Witdongcheon-gil, Dongcheon-dong, Gyeongju-si, Gyeongsangbuk-do

LAKESIDE CAFE

This cafe is located inside the Hilton Gyeongju but you don't have to be a guest to enjoy their extensive breakfast buffet! They've got a wide variety of both Korean and western-style dishes, as well as service you'd expect at a Hilton. It's a great place to start off a day exploring the Bomun Lake area!

🕐 **Open:** 6:30am-10pm

📍 **Where:** Bomun Tourist Complex, by Bomun Lake

🏛 **Address:** 484-7 Bomun-ro, Hilton Gyeongju, Gyeongju, Gyeongsangbuk-do

METDOL SUNDUBU

Start your morning in true South Korean style with some spicy tofu stew! This spot is humble but delicious, and it opens early enough for you to get a jump on the day. They typically don't serve their entire menu for breakfast, but if you fall in love, make sure to stop by later and try more of their classic dishes!

🕐 **Open:** 7am-9:30pm

📍 **Where:** Bomun Tourist Complex

🏛 **Address:** 229-1, Bukgun-dong, Gyeongju, Gyeongsangbuk-do

Lunch

GYEONGJU WONJO KONGGUK

This family-owned and run restaurant is always a favorite with locals! The lunch sets are hearty and filling, and the atmosphere is warm and cozy. Try the traditional soy bean soup and the seafood pajeon (Korean pancake).

⊙ **Open:** 5:30am-8pm

♥ **Where:** Downtown Zone

🏛 **Address:** 113 Cheomseong-ro, Hwangnam-dong, Gyeongju-si, Gyeongsangbuk-do

WITH GUSTO

With Gusto serves up delicious Korean-Italian fusion in a lovely upscale atmosphere. They also serve imported Italian wines and beers.

⊙ **Open:** 11am-9pm

♥ **Where:** Downtown Zone

🏛 **Address:** 1083-2, Poseok-ro, Gyeongju, Gyeongsangbuk-do

GYEONGJU KIMBAP

For a quick, cheap, tasty lunch, stop at this small shop in the Downtown Zone. The owner has developed her own twist on traditional Kimbap, including sesame leaf kimbap and spicy kimbap with a special secret sauce. Get in, get out, get on with your travels!

⊙ **Open:** 8am-7:30pm

♥ **Where:** Downtown Zone

🏛 **Address:** 515-2 Hwangseong-dong, Gyeongju-si, Gyeongsangbuk-do

GIMSSIBEUT

This Asian fusion restaurant is a hidden gem! The friendly staff here doesn't speak much English but they bend over backwards to help you choose the perfect dish. Try the pork and rice bowl or the cream jjamppong (spicy seafood and noodles).

⊙ **Open:** 11am-3pm; 5pm-8pm

♥ **Where:** Downtown Zone

🏛 **Address:** Gyerim-ro 95beon-gil, 6 KR, Gyeongju-si, Gyeongsangbuk-do

JULIE'S

The eclectic western menu at Julie's provides a welcome change if you need a break from Korean fare. From Italian to Indian, the chef prepares everything exquisitely. There's also a pretty patio so you can dine alfresco if the weather is nice.

⊙ **Open:** 11am-9pm

♥ **Where:** Downtown Zone

🏛 **Address:** 20 Sonhyoja-gil, Hwangnam-dong, Gyeongju-si, Gyeongsangbuk-do

Dinner

SURIME

You'll need to make reservations before coming out to this haute restaurant along Gyeongju's southwestern edge. But trust me, it's worth the hassle! The menu is entirely seasonal and treats you to a traditional Korean banquet with multiple courses of perfectly prepared cuisine. The restaurant is in a hanok (traditional Korean house) so you'll feel like you've truly stepped back in time.

⊙ **Open:** 12pm-9pm

♥ **Where:** Seoak

🏛**Address:** 110-32 Poseok-ro, Naenam-myeon, Gyeongju-si, Gyeongsangbuk-do

Pro Tip: The staff here does not speak much, if any, English. You can call from your phone for translation service: 1330 if you have a Korean SIM card or +82-2-1330.

DAEGU GALBI

The menu here is small but very well done, with succulent pork ribs in spicy sauce. If you can't handle a lot of spice, try the pork stew instead. The staff also speaks decent English and are extremely attentive in filling up your side dishes!

⊙ **Open:** 24 hours a day!

♥ **Where:** Downtown Zone

🏛**Address:** 329-3, Hwango-dong, Gyeongju, Gyeongsangbuk-do

HONGSI HANJEONGSIK

Another traditional Korean set restaurant, this is a bit more approachable than Surime. You don't need reservations ahead of time, but you'll still walk away with a truly incredible dining experience. Multiple courses, including ssambap, served in a cozy wood-ensconced setting, finished off with your choice of traditional Korean liquor, of course!

⊙ **Open:** 11:30am-9:30pm

♥ **Where:** Downtown Zone

🏛**Address:** 418-4 Seonggeon-dong, Gyeongju-si, Gyeongsangbuk-do

LUNAR CAT BAR DINER

This little gem of a restaurant offers great steaks and pasta dishes. The owner speaks English and is a professionally trained chef who'll often create something off-menu just for you to try.

⊙ **Open:** 12pm-10pm

♥ **Where:** Downtown Zone

🏛**Address:** 751, Taejong-ro, Gyeongju, Gyeongsangbuk-do 38158

Street Food

Of course, it wouldn't be South Korea without street food! Gyeongju has two great open air markets where you can find dozens of street food vendors selling traditional local dishes.

SEONGDONG MARKET

⊘ *Open:* 8am-7pm

♀ *Where:* Seoak

🏬*Address:* 11, Wonhwa-ro 281beon-gil, Gyeongju, Gyeongsangbuk-do 38146

JUNGANG MARKET

⊘ *Open:* 6am-10:30pm

♀ *Where:* Seoak

🏬*Address:* 295 Geumseong-ro, Seonggeon-dong, Gyeongju-si, Gyeongsangbuk-do

VISITKOREA.OR.KR

Fun Fact!

South Korean wedding attire is typically red, the color of good fortune.

WHERE TO DRINK
IN GYEONGJU

Gyeongju isn't known for its nightlife but there are still a couple fun bars in the more standard western style. Plus, almost every restaurant will serve Korean liquors (think soju and beopju), beer, and wine.

STILLROOM

If you're a whisky cocktail fan, this place is a must! Their cocktails are the real deal, strong and tasty, and extremely reasonably priced. The atmosphere is swanky yet casual and the bartenders really know their stuff.

🕐 **Open:** 11:30am-2am

📍 **Where:** Downtown Zone

🏛 **Address:** 87 Jungbu-dong, Gyeongju-si, Gyeongsangbuk-do

DOMI KITCHEN AND PUB

This super foreigner-friendly pub is always packed with expats and tourists. Hang out and grab some handmade pizza and a local beer or cocktail; their outdoor terrace is especially nice at sunset.

🕐 **Open:** 11am-midnight

📍 **Where:** Downtown Zone

🏛 **Address:** 10, Jungang-ro, Gyeongju, Gyeongsangbuk-do 38158

THINGS TO DO
IN GYEONGJU

EXPERIENCE ANCIENT WAYS OF LIFE IN A TRADITIONAL VILLAGE

Get a taste of what life was like in the Silla Kingdom in one of Gyeongju's two traditional villages.

Yangdong Village is South Korea's largest traditional village complex and has been home to two South Korean families (the Wolseong Son family and the Yeogang Lee family) for over 500 years. You won't find kitschy tourist attractions here - this village is the real deal.

After Yangdong, head on over to Gyochon Hanok Village, where you can try the famous beopju liquor brewed by the Choi family.

💰**Budget:** Free

🏛**Address:** Yangdong: 134 Yangdongmaeul-gil, Gangdong-myeon, Gyeongju-si, Gyeongsangbuk-do / **Gyochon Hanok Village:** 39-2 Gyochon-gil, Gyeongju, Gyeongsangbuk-do

☞ **Getting There:**

◇**Yangdong:** From Gyeongju Station, take Bus 200, 201-208, 212, or 217 to Yangdong Village; it's about a mile walk from there.

◇ **Gyochon Hanok Village:** From the Gyeongju Intercity Bus Terminal, cross the street and get on Bus 61. Take that to the Silla Hoegwan Stop and follow the signs to the village.

HIKE AMID BUDDHIST CARVINGS AND PAGODAS

A morning hike up Mount Namsan in Gyeongju National Park lets you take in both the region's breathtaking natural beauty and its rich culture. The trail is peppered with Buddha sculptures, stone carvings, and gorgeous pagodas. The hike is steep in places so wear proper footwear and bring plenty of water!

If you're not up for a tough hike, Gyeongju National Park is also home to the stunning Anapji (Wolji) Pond - stick around for sunset when the Woljeonggyo Bridge across the pond becomes illuminated.

Budget: Admission varies depending on what you plan to see; plan for about $2-5.

Address: 12 Cheonbungnam-ro, Bodeok-dong, Gyeongju-si, Gyeongsangbuk-do

Getting There: From the Gyeongju Express Bus Terminal, cross the street and get on Bus 11. Ride that 30 stops to the Tammaeul Bus Stop; from there, you can flag a taxi to the park.

VISIT SOUTH KOREA'S FIRST EXPERIENTIAL ZOO

Fair Warning: if birds aren't your thing, you'll want to skip this one. But for you animal lovers, Gyeongju Bird Park is a fun way to spend a few hours getting up close and personal with the animals! There's also a pretty botanical garden and a small cafe on-site.

Budget: $15 for both the zoo and the garden

Address: 74-14, Bomun-ro, Gyeongju, Gyeongsangbuk-do 38117

Getting There: From the Gyeongju Intercity Bus Terminal, cross the street and take Bus 10 or 700 to the Donggungwon Entrance Bus Stop.

CARB UP ON LOCAL TREATS

In a country chock full of tasty and quirky sweets, Gyeongju takes the, well, bread. Keep your eyes peeled for the city's famous Hwangnam bread, small pillowy pastries filled with sweet red bean paste. The dish was created in Gyeongju in the 1930s, and which bakery makes the best remains a hotly debated local topic.

💰Budget: $2-5

🏠Address: Just about any local sweet shop, particularly in the Downtown Zone.

GET YOUR THRILLS AT GYEONGJU WORLD

Need a break from temples and tombs? Get in touch with your inner child at Gyeongju World, one of South Korea's largest theme parks. Have a blast playing Korean arcade and carnival games. Thrill-seekers will love the X-Zone area, with roller coasters with names like Mega Drop and Tornado. You can also soak up the sun at California Beach water park in the summer and a huge sledding hill in the winter. And of course, there are tons of eating and shopping options nearby.

💰Budget: $19 for admission and another $35 for a ride pass

🏠Address:544, Bomun-ro, Gyeongju-si, Gyeongsangbuk-do

☞ Getting There: From the Gyeongju Intercity Bus Terminal, get on bus 10 or 100 toward the Bomun Tourist Complex and get off at the Gyeongju World Bus Stop.

TAKE PART IN A TRADITIONAL SOUTH KOREAN TEA CEREMONY

Indulge like Silla royalty with a traditional tea ceremony in one of Gyeongju's historic tea houses! You can find teahouses in pretty much all of the major tourist areas, and Golgulsa Temple and Bulguksa Temple also offer tea ceremonies.

Budget: Plan for $10-20

STROLL THROUGH DAEREUNGWON TUMULI PARK

Located in the middle of Gyeongju's historic city center, this 37-acre park consists of dozens of massive tumuli, manicured burial mounds built for the ancient city's rich leaders. Several of the tombs have been excavated, giving you a peek inside Silla burial culture.

Budget: $1.50

Address: 9 Gyerim-ro, Hwangnam-dong, Gyeongju-si, Gyeongsangbuk-do

Getting There: From the Gyeongju Intercity Bus Terminal, get on Bus 10, 11, or 70. These will take you to the park's front gate.

South Korea Notes...

....

....

....

....

....

....

....

Sightseeing

BULGUKSA TEMPLE

This UNESCO World Cultural Heritage Site showcases a host of national treasures and represents the epitome of Buddhist architecture. Walk past the statues of the Four Heavenly Kings at the entrance gates and stand in awe under brightly tiled roofs. Take in the famous Dabotap and Seokgatap pagodas and catch temple monks performing age-old Buddhist rituals. The temple also offers an overnight temple stay program to truly immerse yourself in its rich history.

🖉 *Budget:* $4.20 for both Bulguksa Temple and Seokguram Grotto (see below)

♀ *Where:* 385, Bulguk-ro, Gyeongju-si, Gyeongsangbuk-do

⊙ *Open:* 7am-6pm

GYEONGJU NATIONAL MUSEUM

Make this one of your first stops in Gyeongju to learn everything about ancient Silla. The museum houses over 80,000 artifacts, including jewelry, weapons, calligraphy, and artwork. Be sure to check out the Emille Bell, one of the world's oldest and largest bronze bells. Its name means "mummy" in the ancient Silla language, and it's said that its toll sounds like a lost child crying for its mother.

☉ **Open:** 9am-6pm; closed Mondays

💸**Budget:** Free (although you will be given an admission ticket to enter)

♥ **Where:** 186 Il Jeong-ro, Wolseong-dong, Gyeongju-si, Gyeongsangbuk-do (inside Gyeongju National Park)

SEOKGURAM GROTTO

From Bulguksa, you can take a short bus ride (or longer hike) to Seokguram Grotto, where you'll find a massive granite statue of the Buddha that's considered one of the most unique pieces of Asian Buddhist art still in existence. The South Korean government has encased the statue in thick pieces of glass in order to preserve it, but even through glass, it's an astounding site.

💸**Budget:** $4.20 combo ticket for the Grotto and Bulguksa

☉ **Open:** 6:30am-6pm

♥ **Where:** Jinhyeon-dong, Gyeongju-si, Gyeongsangbuk-do

GOLGULSA TEMPLE

Even if you're feeling a little templed-out, you do not want to miss this third beauty! Explore 12 caves carved into the cliff-face of Hamwolsan Mountain, with Buddhist sculptures sprinkled throughout and a massive Buddha statue overlooking it all. Golgulsa is also famous for Sunmudo, a Korean form of martial arts; you can watch demonstrations and even take lessons as part of their temple stay program.

💸**Budget:** Free (except for the temple stay program)

☉ **Open:** 6am-5pm; cultural performance takes place every day except Monday at 3:30pm

♥ **Where:** 101-5, Girim-ro, Yangbuk-myeon, Gyeongju-si, Gyeongsangbuk-do

CHEOMSEONGDAE

Visit this site in the heart of Gyeongju's historic center to see the oldest existing astronomical observatory in East Asia. Cheomseongdae was built in the 7th century and while it might not look particularly fancy, it's an impressive testament to Korea's scientific history.

As a bonus, Cheomseongdae is also surrounded by a beautiful park where locals often come to picnic in hanboks.

⊙ **Open:** 9am-9pm

🖊**Budget:** Free

📍 **Where:** 839-1 Inwang-dong, Gyeongju-si, Gyeongsangbuk-do

KING MUNMU'S UNDERWATER TOMB

Trek a little further off the beaten path to Bonggil Daewangam Beach and look out to sea, where you'll see a small rocky island. This is the tomb of King Munmu, who requested that he be buried underwater so that he could come back as a dragon to protect South Korea from Japanese invasion. You'll often find locals performing traditional Shaman rituals on the shore. And don't skip on all the delicious seafood restaurants and food stalls lining the beach!

⊙ **Open:** 24 hours a day

🖊**Budget:** Free

📍 **Where:** Bonggil-ri Ap Haejung, Yangbuk-myeon, Gyeongju-si, Gyeongsangbuk-do

Fun Fact!

In terms of land size, South Korea is about the size of Indiana.

SHOPPING
IN GYEONGJU

GYEONGJU FOLK CRAFT VILLAGE

Walk through 40 beautiful thatched-roof houses inhabited by traditional local artisans. The village has everything from pottery and metalwork to jewelry and hanboks. Some of the shops offer demonstrations or even hands-on classes. This is the perfect spot to grab some one-of-a-kind gifts for your friends and family - and yourself!

♥ *Where:* 230, Bobul-ro, Gyeongju-si, Gyeongsangbuk-do

JUNGANG MARKET

Jungang Market is the main market for Gyeongju's locals. It's packed with over 700 stalls selling clothes, oils, vegetables, rice cakes, household goods, and more. The night market boasts a boatload of street food stalls, plus a ton of tables and seating on the street. Grab a couple beers from the nearby convenience store and settle in!

♥ *Where:* 295 Geumseong-ro, Seonggeon-dong, Gyeongju-si, Gyeongsangbuk-do

SEONGDONG MARKET

During the day, Seongdong Market sells souvenirs, clothes, and traditional South Korean goods. It's located opposite of the train station, making it a convenient last stop before you head out of the city. And of course, after dark, it turns into a bustling street food area!

Address: 11, Wonhwa-ro 281beon-gil, Gyeongju, Gyeongsangbuk-do 38146

CHAPTER FIVE

Jeju Island

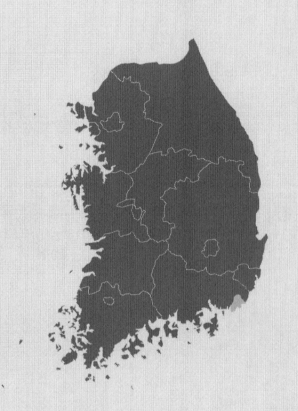

Jeju Island

INTRODUCTION TO JEJU ISLAND

Time to slow down and unwind from the craziness of the big cities with a trip to South Korea's "honeymoon island." Jeju Island was created by volcanic eruptions millions of years ago, and today it's home to a lush landscape rife with beauty and relaxation. Come sink your toes into the sand!

Treat yourself to fruity cocktails, luxurious massages, and invigorating Korean body scrubs at one of the island's many resorts and spas. Beach hop along white sand shores with turquoise blue waves. Gorge yourself on delicious fresh seafood and tangerines straight from the tree and learn about Jeju's famous haenyeo - women free-divers who spend their days gathering seafood with nothing but a knife and their own lung power.

Stroll along country lanes lined with black lava rocks. If you're feeling more active, rent some snorkel or diving gear and take in the beautiful colored coral and vibrant sea life. Or get out for a hike along Halla-san, South Korea's highest mountain, or Seongsan Ilchul-bong, Jeju's famous "Sunrise Peak."

Whatever your vacation flavor, Jeju Island will be a trip to remember!

Getting There from the Mainland

By Air

There are a ton of domestic flights coming into Jeju from both Seoul and Busan, so it's easy to hop on over from the mainland by air!

♥ Where: Jeju National Airport is located about 2.5 miles outside of the main city center (Jeju City).

When: There are flights from Gimpo Airport and Gimhae Airport to Jeju island every 5 to 15 minutes. Flights from Gimpo (GMP) to (and from) Jeju (CJU) is the busiest domestic route in the world, with about 80,000 flights a year. One way flight to Jeju will cost around $10-90 depending on schedule and date.

How Much: Flights will cost anywhere from $100-200

By Ferry

For a more adventurous trip, hop on a ferry from one of the mainland ports. The most popular option is the overnight ferry from Busan's Domestic Ferry Terminal, but you can also catch boats from Incheon Port Coast Passenger Terminal (near Seoul).

♥ Where: Catch the ferry from Busan or Incheon and you'll land at Jeju Ferry Terminal 1 (domestic terminal).

◊**From Seoul:** Take Subway Line 1 from Seoul Station to Dongincheon Station and leave through Exit 2. Walk to the McDonalds and get on Bus 12 or 24 to the terminal.

◊**From Busan:** Take Subway Line 1 to Busan Station; get on Bus 1004 for two stops OR walk about 10 minutes.

⊙ When: Ferries run a few times per week; the trip will take between 11-14 hours.

How Much: For normal ferries, fares will run you from $29 for the lowest class to $180 for a VIP room.

Getting Around Jeju Island

By Bus

There are no subway or train lines on Jeju Island so the bus will be your go-to for public transportation. There are two types of buses on Jeju:

◇ **City Buses:** Intercity buses run between the main Jeju and Seogwipo terminals with several stops in between. Blue buses are regular buses, while red buses are express buses that connect the airport and bus terminals. Bus 201 runs along the east coast of the island, while Bus 202 runs along the west coast.

How Much: $1-1.50 for regular fare; $2-2.50 for express fare

◇ **Airport Limousine Buses:** It's easy to hop on this bus straight from the airport. You can catch the bus outside the arrivals area at Gate 1 (or Gate 5 if you land after 10:30pm).

📎 **How Much:** It will cost about $5 to get into the city.

Pro Tip: With your T-money card, you get two free transfers within 40 minutes on Jeju intercity buses.

By Taxi

Getting around Jeju by bus may be cheap, but you'll obviously be constrained by schedules. Grabbing a taxi instead can eliminate waiting around at bus stops and also deliver you door-to-door between your hotel and your next destination. You can grab a taxi in Jeju at the airport or major bus station, or just flag them down on the street.

📎 **How Much:** Surprisingly affordable! Fares start at about $2.50 for the first 1.25 miles, and you can go around 9 miles for about 10.

Pro Tip: Taxis stop running around 10pm if you're anywhere outside of downtown Jeju City. Be prepared!

....

By Car

For even more freedom, rent a car or hire a private driver. There are car rental places at both the airport and the ferry terminal. Either option will obviously cost you more than the bus or a couple of taxis, but if you have a big itinerary planned for a day, it can be worth it to save the hassle!

🖉 **How Much:** Renting a car will cost you about $50-70 a day, while a private driver can start at $150 a day.

....

By Bike/Scooter

If the weather's nice, explore some of the island on a bike or scooter! There are dedicated cycleways in a lot of areas, meaning you can relax and enjoy the scenery without having to worry about dodging cars. Bikes and scooters can be rented in Jeju City and Seogwipo.

🖉 **How Much:** Bikes cost about $8.50 a day to rent, while scooters cost $12-20 a day.

Pro Tip: If you rent a car OR a scooter, you'll need to get your international driver's license in advance (stop at your local AAA before your trip!). You also need to be at least 21 years old.

Fun Fact!

South Korea has one of the least obese populations in the world.

Neighborhoods in Jeju Island

JEJU CITY

This is the main area on Jeju Island and is a great place to get a taste of the island! It has the white sand beaches, the delicious food, the shopping and historic sites, and the breathtaking natural landscape. If you don't have long to stay on Jeju Island, Jeju City should definitely be your first stop!

SEOGWIPO CITY

Located on Jeju Island's southern coast, Seogwipo is known for its laid-back vibe and its budget-friendly hotels and dining. This area is also one of the best places to experience waterfalls, volcanic craters, and all the rest of Jeju Island's stunning natural treasures.

JUNGMUN

Jungmun is technically part of Seogwipo, but it deserves its own mention here as one of Jeju Island's main tourist areas. Here is where you'll find gorgeous luxury resorts, museums, and tours catering to foreign visitors. Plan to stop here for some of the best seafood on the island as well!

AEWOL

Home to two of Jeju's most famous beaches, Aewol is a great spot to while away some time relaxing on the sand or going snorkeling or paddle boarding. There's also a beautiful park famous for its gardens and folk village, as well as a plethora of restaurants and cafes dotting the seaside.

WHERE TO STAY IN JEJU ISLAND

GOLDONE HOTEL AND SUITES

One of the fanciest hotels on Jeju Island where spoiling yourself comes easy. Kick back in style at this 4-star hotel right on the beach in Seogwipo City. You can enjoy your own private hot tub plus a gorgeous outdoor pool overlooking the ocean. There's also a beautiful rooftop garden space and a delicious buffet breakfast.

💸 **Budget:** $$$$

☆ **Style:** Private rooms

📍 **Where:** Beachfront in Seogwipo

🏫 **Address:** 1032, Ieodo-ro, Seogwipo City, 63571 Seogwipo

 BOOK HERE

LEMAIN HOTEL

Walk to the beach! Walk through the village! Take your book on a date to a nearby cafe! Walk to Hallim Park or a bar or a restaurant! You are completely independent here. No car or scooter needed. Most rooms have a sea view and are totally worth the price.

💸 **Budget:** $$$

☆ **Style:** Private Rooms

📍 **Where:** Hyeopjae Beach

 BOOK HERE

THE SEAES HOTEL AND RESORT

Hello, private pool villas and beautiful sea views from your own balcony at The Seaes! This stunning property has actually been featured in multiple Korean movies. You can also pamper yourself at the on-site sauna and spa and enjoy a sunset cocktail on the gorgeous outdoor lounge. This is my top Jeju hotel pick!

Budget: $$

Style: Private room

Where: Center of Jungmun tourist area

Address: 198, Jungmungwangwang-ro, Jungmun Beach

 BOOK HERE

JEJU STARLIGHT GLAMPING

A once-in-a-lifetime experience where you can choose to sleep in a bubble glamping tent or a modern RV in Jeju. Wi-Fi is weak here...enjoy it! Take a dip in the small pool with a view of the ocean or lay out under the stars at night! Here is where you come to unplug on the other side of the world, my babe. The location is in the middle of nowhere so you'll need to arrange a ride with the hotel before you come.

💵 *Budget:* $$

☆ *Style:* Quirky Rooms

📍 *Where:* Aewol

🏠 *Address:* 348, Gwangsang-ro, Aewol-eup, Aewol

 BOOK HERE

SEA AND BIKE

Off the beaten path! If you want to get away from the locals on vacation, this is where you stay. But don't worry, there are plenty of little seaside cafes within walking distance and you can rent a bike here for 10,000W. The guesthouse itself has an on-site restaurant and lounge, complete with dart board for playing and a lovely terrace for relaxing. You will be well taken care of here.

💵 *Budget:* $$

☆ *Style:* Dorms and Privates

📍 *Where:* Aewol, right on the beach

🏠 *Address:* 42, Gonae-ro 9-gil, Aewol-eup

 BOOK HERE

YEHA GUESTHOUSE

Be in the heart of it all at Yeha Guesthouse. Don't waste your time commuting- you'll be able to get here quickly from the airport, train, or bus station so you can hit the ground running! You'll also get free rice and kimchi, as well as one free drink at happy hour. If you're short on time, this is where I recommend you stay!

Budget: $$

☆**Style:** Dorms and Privates

♥ **Where:** Central Jeju City, minutes from main transportation hubs and dining

Address: 9 Samo-gil, Jeju City, 63185 Jeju

 BOOK HERE

HANNAHSTAY WOMEN-ONLY GUESTHOUSE

Meet some other solo female travelers at this bright, homey guesthouse! You are bound to meet some other Korean girls while you're eating breakfast (which is the best ever) or hanging in your dorm room. Just 20 minutes from the airport, Hannahstay is another convenient place to stay if you plan to take public transportation to explore the island!

Budget: $

☆**Style:** Dorms and Privates

♥ **Where:** Jeju City

Address: 6, Gwangyang 1-gil, Jeju City, 63197

 BOOK HERE

"WHEREVER YOU GO BECOMES A PART OF YOU SOMEHOW"

- Anita Desai

WHERE TO EAT
IN JEJU ISLAND

Breakfasts & Coffee Shops

ESPRESSON LOUNGE

This spacious espresso bar offers a ton of seating, a welcoming vibe, and good coffee! You can also get freshly made sandwiches and pastries. It's conveniently located in the downtown Jeju City, making it easy to pop in and out.

⊙ *Open:* 9am-10pm
♥ *Where:* Jeju City
🛗*Address:* 1, Halladaehak-ro, Jeju-si, Jeju-do

BAUM: JEJU COFFEE MUSEUM

Start in the "experience room" where you can learn about coffee roasting

and see the beans being prepared. Then move to the lounge or rooftop terrace and enjoy a freshly brewed espresso, latte, or drip coffee.

⊙ *Open:* 9:30am-6:30pm Mon-Thurs; 10am-7pm Fri-Sun
♥ *Where:* Seogwipo
🛗*Address:* 89-17, Seoseongil-ro 1168beon-gil, Seongsan-eup | 2f, Jeju, Jeju Island

HOBONG FOOD

This hole-in-the-wall stand is a great place to grab yummy toasted sandwiches and coffee to go. Try the cheese toast or the sweet potato egg toast!

⊙ *Open:* 9am-9pm
♥ *Where:* Jeju City
🛗*Address:* 56, Ujeong-Ro, Jeju, Jeju Island

UJIN HAEJANGGUK

Home to South Korea's famed hangover stew, this restaurant is the perfect breakfast spot even if you aren't suffering from the night before. There's an English menu detailing all their delicious soups, and you'll get a truly authentic South Korean experience with the ajummas calling out the numbers and serving you!

⊘ *Open:* 6am-10pm

♀ *Where:* Jeju City

🚇 *Address:* 11 Seosa-ro, Samdo 2(i)-dong, Jeju-si, Jeju-do

MYEONGJIN JEONBOK ABALONE RESTAURANT

If you want to get your first taste of abalone, this is one of the best places to go. Super affordable (for abalone), big portions, and different preparations to choose from. You'll even get a mackerel side dish with your meal which, in my opinion, is almost as good as the star of the show!

⊘ *Open:* 9:30am-9:30pm; closed Tuesdays

♀ *Where:* Jeju City

🚇 *Address:* 1282 Haemajihaean-ro, Gujwa-eup, Jeju-si, Jeju-do

Lunch

AND YU CAFÉ

This British-Korean cafe is 100% vegan and 100% delicious! Veggie burgers, soups, smoothies, kombucha, and desserts - you'll walk away feeling full and healthy!

⊘ *Open:* 11am-7pm Thurs-Mon

♀ *Where:* Jeju City

🚇 *Address:* 518 Hallim-ro | Ongpo-ri, Hallim-eup, Jeju, Jeju, Jeju Island

MEXICO MACHO GRILL

This hidden gem offers delicious Mexican food with a Korean twist! Try the carnitas burrito and of course, the kimchi fries, and wash it down with a margarita or ice-cold beer.

⊘ *Open:* 11am-10pm; closed Mondays

♀ *Where:* Jeju City

🚇 *Address:* 39, Joongang-ro | 2F, Jeju, Jeju Island

Dinnner

MODICA ITALIAN RESTAURANT

You'll find authentic Italian fare with a beautiful ambience at Modica. Prices are a little higher than other restaurants but it's a beautiful place for a splurge.

☉ *Open:* 6pm-10pm for dinner

♥ *Where:* Aewol

🏛 *Address:* 905-19 Hanrim-ri, Hallim-eub, Jeju-si, Jeju-do

DASONI

Come to this Buddhist vegetarian restaurant for beautiful local dishes prepared perfectly. It's a traditional teahouse, meaning you'll remove your shoes and sit cross-legged on the floor, which just adds to its charm!

☉ *Open:* 11am-8pm; closed Sundays

♥ *Where:* Jeju City

🏛 *Address:* 24 Onam-ro 6-gil, Orail-dong, Jeju-si, Jeju-do

MINT

Enjoy stunning views from Mint's floor-to-ceiling windows overlooking the water! If you're looking for a high-end night out, this is a great place to start. They serve high-quality local dishes like black pork and abalone, as well as more fusion-type dishes like squid ink risotto. Expect to pay more for the view!

☉ *Open:* 10am-9pm

♥ *Where:* Seogwipo

🏛 *Address:* 107, Seopjikoji-ro, Seongsan-eup | Phoenix Island Glass House 2F, Seogwipo, Jeju Island

HAEJIN SEAFOOD RESTAURANT

This is one of Jeju's most popular spots to try local seafood like abalone, sea cucumber, urchin, and octopus. It overlooks Jeju Harbor and offers an extensive variety of seafood prepared both grilled and sashimi-style.

☉ *Open:* 10:30am-midnight

♥ *Where:* Jeju City

🏛 *Address:* 1435-2 Geonip-dong, Jeju-si, Jeju-do

Fun Fact!

K-pop is the country's third largest export.

WHERE TO DRINK IN JEJU ISLAND

SURF BAR GOOFY FOOT

This chill bar is a perennial favorite among tourists with its extensive craft beer list and pool tables and dartboards. The bartenders are friendly and the crowd is typically very laid back and low-key.

⊙ **Open:** 6:30pm-3am

♥ **Where:** Jeju City

🏢 **Address:** 11 Gwangyang 10-gil, Idoi-dong, Jeju-do Jeju-si

BLUEBIRD BY MAGPIE

Another popular craft beer spot, Bluebird by Magpie (otherwise known as Magpie Jeju) has a hipster vibe and a long list of brews by both local and international breweries. Their fried chicken also makes a great late-night snack!

⊙ **Open:** 5pm-1am

♥ **Where:** Jeju City

🏢 **Address:** 7, Tapdong-ro 2-gil, Jeju, Jeju Island

THE FACTORY

Locals and tourists alike flock to The Factory to relax with a beer or whiskey and listen to live music. It's got a hipster vibe and tends to attract artistic types and definitely has a chill, low-key vibe.

⊙ **Open:** 7pm-2am Sat-Sun

♥ **Where:** Jeju City

🏢 **Address:** 1180-1 Ido 2-dong, Jeju-do Jeju-si

INDIE

Jeju Island isn't a very "clubby" place, but this is the bar to head to if you feel like dancing! The music trends toward metal and heavy rock.

🕐 *Open:* 8pm-2am; closed Sundays

📍 *Where:* Jeju City

🏛 *Address:* 301 1189-11 beon-gil, Block B, Ido 2-dong, Jeju-do Jeju-si

CAFE MAY-B

If you've had enough beer and are in the mood for a cocktail or glass of wine, this is your place! Cafe May-B has a quieter atmosphere than some of Jeju's other more divey bars, and it's really foreigner-friendly.

🕐 *Open:* 10:30am-1am

📍 *Where:* Seogwipo

🏛 *Address:* 478-12 Seogwi-dong, Seogwipo-si, Jeju-do

THE SOLO GIRL'S

Travel Academy

Have you ever wanted to just pack it all up and go?

Travel the world solo, escape the monotony of the 9–5, and trade the politics for purpose.

That's what I did.
And now, I'm teaching you how to do the same.

Join me at SoloGirlsTravelAcademy.com

THINGS TO DO
IN JEJU ISLAND

JEJU ISLAND PHOTO TOUR

What better way to remember your visit to Jeju Island forever than with some gorgeous professional photos? This tour will take you to some spectacular sites in Seogwipo, where the professional photographer will snap your photo amidst the picturesque background.

☆*Style:* Private (you can bring up to 7 friends though!)

Budget: $46

☉ *Open:* 1.5 hours

GO BEACH-HOPPING

When most people think of Jeju, they think beaches - and it's obvious why! The island's amazing pristine beaches are the perfect spot to relax and refresh. Jeju Island's most popular beaches include:

◊ **Iho Taewoo Beach:** Near downtown Jeju City, famous for its unique yellow-gray sand and its horse-shaped lighthouse

◊ **Hamdeok Beach:** Jeju City, huge area with three separate beaches, plus a ton of restaurants and shops

◊ **Gwakji Beach:** Near Aewol, huge sandy beach with crystal-clear water and a cold-water spring

◊ **Hyeopjae Beach:** Southern end of Aewol, shallower water than other beaches, gorgeous view at sunset

◊ **Jungmun Beach:** Southeastern end of Seogwipo on Jeju's southern coast, surrounded by luxury resorts and high-end dining

◊ **Hado Beach:** On Jeju's northern tip and a bit harder to get to, great for kayaking or paddle boarding; also, a good place to watch haenyeo at work!

Budget: Free!

VISIT A WATERFALL

Jeju is home to tons of stunning waterfalls - it's known as the Hawaii of Korea! Even if you're not a mega outdoorsy person, it's worth your time to take in at least one of these gorgeous falls. Four of the most beautiful on Jeju Island are:

◊ **Jeongbang:** The only waterfall in Asia to fall straight into the ocean!

◊ **Cheonjiyeon:** The name means "sky connected with land" and the path to the waterfall has tons of rare subtropical plants and trees.

◊ **Cheonjeyeon:** Three-tiered waterfall surrounded by a lush park

◊ **Wonang Falls:** at the foot of Hallasan, known for its crystal-clear, freezing cold water

Budget: About $1.50 entrance fee to the parks

Pro Tip: The rocks surrounding waterfalls get super slippery so don't wear flip flops!

GO FOR A HIKE

Another way to take in Jeju's breathtaking volcanic landscape is to hike one of its many peaks. If you're feeling adventurous, head to Hallasan (South Korea's tallest mountain) for a four-hour climb or to Seongsan Ilchul-bong (Sunrise Peak) for a slightly less challenging trek. For something a little more leisurely, wander along the Jeju Olle walking trails; be sure not to miss Suwolbong Peak, an inactive volcanic cone with a gorgeous view!

TRY ABALONE, BLACK PORK, AND SEA CUCUMBER

Foodies won't want to miss Jeju's most famous local delicacies!

Abalone is typically insanely expensive but on Jeju, you can find it for a steal! Try it thin-sliced and raw, grilled, or my favorite, in a rice porridge (jeonbukjuk).

Heak dwaeji is Jeju's famed black pork, a succulent meat from pigs bred exclusively on the island. You'll smell this deliciousness grilling everywhere!

Feeling more adventurous? Give sea cucumber (haesam) a try! It's not a vegetable - it's actually a sea creature with a chewy texture and a slightly salty taste. It's often served raw with chili paste or in seafood stews.

WATCH A HAENYEO DIVE SHOW

Get ready for some major girl power! Haenyeo are Jeju's incredible women free divers - these real-life mermaids dive to the ocean floor by holding their breath and use only a knife to collect abalone, sea cucumbers, urchins, seaweed, and other seafood! Many of these divers are well into their 70s, and the tradition is so important to Jeju and to Korea as a whole that the haenyeo have been declared a UNESCO Intangible Cultural Heritage of Humanity.

Watch their incredible feats at the Sea Women Restaurant or House of Women Diver, near Seongsan Ilchul-bong.

Budget: Around $2

⊙ *Open:* Shows at 1:30pm and 3pm

Pro Tip: If you see a haenyeo show, understand that it's not for entertainment - these women are going about their normal jobs so are not there to interact with the tourists. That being said, it's an incredible thing to see, and you can usually buy a plate of the freshest seafood of your life after the show!

Sightseeing

LOVE LAND

Welcome to what might just be the world's dirtiest theme park! Love Land is an adults-only sculpture park dedicated to sex. Leave your inhibitions at the door and take goofy photos with some of the most salacious statues you'll ever see!

🕐 **Open:** 9am-midnight

💸 **Budget:** Around $9

🏛 **Address:** 2894-72 1100(Cheonbaek)-ro, Yeon-dong, Jeju-si, Jeju-do

SHOPPING IN JEJU ISLAND

JUNGANG UNDERGROUND SHOPPING CENTER

It's easy to get lost in this sprawling underground mall! Luckily you'll have plenty to do and see as you find your way back out. From cosmetics and skincare to clothes, shoes, bags, toys, and household items - if you're in need of basically anything at all, you'll find it here.

⊙ **Open:** 10am-9:30pm

Address: 60, Jungang-ro, Jeju, Jeju Island

DONGMUN TRADITIONAL MARKET

Dongmun is Jeju's best-known fish and seafood market, packed with vendors and seafood restaurants and food stalls. But it has more than just fish! You can also find a ton of local produce, crafts, and locally produced souvenirs. It's also close to the airport, making it a good last stop before heading to the airport.

⊙ **Open:** 8am-9pm; closed Sundays

Address: 20 Gwandeok-ro 14-gil, Jeju-do Jeju-si

JEJU FIVE-DAY FOLK MARKET

This is the biggest traditional market in Jeju. Spend your morning wandering among over a thousand stalls of produce, fish, crafts, and more. Get your fortune read and enjoy a traditional cup of tea. This market is also a "grandma market", or Halmang Jangteo, where women over the age of 65 can sell their wares without needing to rent a stall.

As the name suggests, this market is only open five days per month: the 2, 7, 12, 17, 22, and 27.

⊘ **Open:** 8am-6pm

🏛**Address:** 6 Oiljangseo-gil, Doduil-dong, Jeju-si, Jeju-do

DONAM MARKET

Come to this traditional clothing market if you're looking to buy a hanbok or another piece of traditional Korean garb. In addition to inexpensive clothes, you'll also find a ton of cheap restaurants and cute cafes. It's also a perfect spot to view cherry blossoms in the spring!

⊘ **Open:** 7am-10pm; closed the first and third Sundays of the month

🏛**Address:** 923-13 Donam-dong, Jeju-do Jeju-si

SEOGWIPO MAEIL OLLE MARKET

Live seafood, fresh fruits and vegetables, and abundant street food make this the perfect stop if you're famished after a waterfall hike! Olle Market is also a good place to grab some killer deals on local souvenirs.

⊘ **Open:** 7am-9pm

🏛**Address:** 22 Jungjeong-ro73beon-gil, Seogwi-dong, Seogwipo-si, Jeju-do

South Korea Notes...

....

....

....

....

....

CHAPTER SIX

—

Off-The-Beaten Path

—

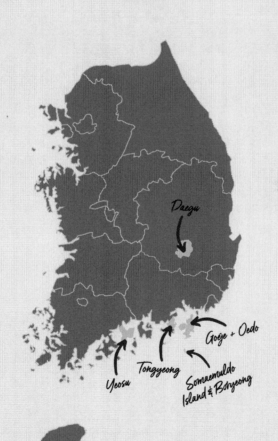

Daegu

Goje + Oedo

Tongyeong

Yeosu

Somaemuldo
Island & Boryeong

INTRODUCTION TO OFF-THE BEATEN PATH SOUTH KOREA

GEOJE + OEDO

If you're in South Korea for any substantial amount of time, you'll definitely want to go island-hopping and hit these gems. Nicknamed "Blue City," Geoje is South Korea's second largest island and is filled with stunning natural coastlines, pine-filled hiking trails, and delectable local seafood. The island is accessible from Busan by car and bus.

From Geoje, hop on a ferry to nearby Oedo Island, South Korea's botanical wonder. The island is privately owned, and its owners have turned the entire thing into a pristinely manicured botanical garden. Don't miss the Stairway to Heaven, which will give you stunning ocean views framed by lush rare flowers.

◇ *Stay here:* Travel Sketch Pension

TONGYEONG

The water world with amazing local seafood delicacies. Tongyeong is particularly famous for oysters and anchovies, plus the famous Tongyeong honey bread, a sweet dough filled with various fillings and glazed with honey-sesame. The island is filled with quaint villages, traditional markets, and beautiful local art. It's accessible from Geoje by car and bus.

◇ *Stay here:* Bella Guesthouse

YEOSU

This southern port town makes a great weekend trip, offering beaches, parks, and sightseeing. Hike up to Hyangiram Temple or take the Maritime Cable Car to nearby Dolsan Island (choose the "crystal car" for a glass-bottomed view of the ocean!). Thrill-seekers can go paragliding, or you can just eat your way through the city's many seafood restaurants. Yeosu is accessible from other major cities by train or bus.

◊ *Stay here:* Seasidepine Pension

SOMAEMULDO ISLAND (소매물도)

Sharp cliffs, crashing waves, and dramatic rock formations - this island is a hiker's paradise! Wander along countless trails from the ferry port up to the island's various peaks. At low tide, you can also walk across the land bridge connecting Somaemuldo to nearby Deungdaeseom Island (Lighthouse Island), home to one of South Korea's most photographed lighthouses. Stop for lunch or a post-hike snack at the many mom-and-pop seafood restaurants dotting the island. Somaemuldo is accessible by ferry from Geoje or Tongyeong.

BORYEONG

Pencil some time into your July calendar for this one - you do not want to miss the annual Boryeong Mud Festival! The festival started as a way to celebrate and promote skincare products made from the region's mud (said to be rich in beneficial minerals), but it quickly morphed into hilarious mud-filled debauchery. Mud wrestling, mud sliding, mud swimming . . . I guarantee you've never seen anything like it! If you choose not to get dirty (although come on, you should absolutely join in!), there are still a ton of parades, cultural demonstrations, vendors, and fireworks shows to keep you entertained.

◊ *Stay here:* Hotel Wooyeon Flora

DAEGU

Daegu is the 4th largest city in Korea but often skipped by travelers...but Daegu is actually one of my favorite cities in Korea. I lived here for one year and enjoyed the downtown culture with amazing shopping and even more amazing goods. There is a large expat/English teacher population here so it was easy to make friends. There's great hiking, a baseball team and a subway system that makes exploring the city extremely easy. I highly recommend a visit here if you've got the time.

◊ *Stay here:* Rivertain Hotel

Fun Fact!

South Korean men must serve in the military for 21-24 months before they reach the age of 30.

ITINERARIES FOR

South Korea

—

You've got two choices when it comes to planning this trip.

1. Try to see it ALL, rush through everything, and be so absolutely exhausted and broke in the end.

2. Create a bucket list that gives you a loose itinerary that allows you to see the best sights without rushing or feeling overwhelmed.

When I'm planning a trip to a new country, I like to make a bucket list rather than a strict schedule. Instead of pressuring myself to "see it all," I pick my must-sees and build my itinerary around those, while leaving room for life to surprise me!

Obsessed with food? Make a list of your bucket list dishes or street food markets. Love Korean culture? Pick your top temples, palaces, and museums. Then let the rest fall into place.

To give you some structure, however, I've created a few itineraries that you can easily follow. Feel free to swap one market for another or one museum for a temple. But this will be a good place for you to start planning!

Here are a few itineraries to get you started!

Pssst...Want me to plan your trip for you?
Alexa-West.com/Services

ONE WEEK: *Seoul*

DAY 1: FLY INTO INCHEON ···

A.M.
→ Head to your hotel in Itaewon
→ Shower, unwind
→ Hit the streets to explore aimlessly.
→ Be spontaneous and fuel up on street food around your hotel.
P.M.
→ Walk to Namsan Park
→ So up to Seoul Tower and watch the sunset.
→ Ease into Korean food with Korean fusion for dinner at Vatos Urban Tacos
→ If you've got the energy, go for a drink at Flower Gin.

DAY 2 ···

A.M.
→ Grab a coffee at Anthracite Coffee Hannam while you revisit this book
→ Hop on a bus to Bukchon Hanok Village
→ Walk around and look for a place that rents Hanbok (the traditional Korean dresses and dress-up).
→ Once you're dressed, explore the complex grounds for culture and another caffeine pick-me-up

P.M.
→ Put your normal clothes back on and walk 10 minutes to Gyeongbokgung Palace to explore
→ Take a Taxi to Gwanghwamun Jip for dinner - order the Kimchi Stew
→ Walk to Sanchez Makgeolli and try the alcoholic Makgeolli
→ Pop into Good Thai Massage Itaewon for a foot massage or a full massage
→ Grab some snacks from 7-Eleven and head back to your hotel for a night in with weird snacks in bed.

DAY 3: SPA DAY ···

A.M.
→ Wake up slow (and hungover)

→Grab breakfast at Root Everyday
→Spend the whole day at Dragon Hill Spa - get massages, scrubs, sleep in the sleeping room, eat - everything!

P.M.
→Head back home to collapse in your hotel room!
→Freshen up a bit and go searching for street food or get in a taxi and wander (and eat) your way through Dongdaemun Night Market

DAY 4: HONGDAE

A.M.
→Take a Taxi to your new hotel in Hongdae
→Grab some downtime at your hotel - enjoy being on vacation!

P.M.
→Head back to Hongdae to hit Hongdae Walking Street for the ultimate shopping
→Pass by Tokkijung Project, if there is no line, go there for dinner. If there is a line, go eat all the street food you can find.
→Go on the Pub Crawl Tour and make some new friends - or make your own DIY pub crawl tour by aimlessly wandering Itaewon starting at Rabbithole Arcade Pub.

DAY 5:

A.M.
→Go on a DMZ tour.

P.M.
→Join a street food tour!

DAY 6: TEMPLE STAY

A.M.
→ Head to check into Jingwansa's temple stay program
→ Spend the night here to relax and reflect before heading home

DAY 7: HOME TIME

→From the temple stay, pack up your belongings and head to the airport.

ONE WEEK: *Seoul & Busan*

(...THIS IS THE MOST PERFECT ITINERARY I'VE EVER MADE!)

◊ *Week One* - Follow the Itinerary Above

◊ *Week Two* - Busan

*Before planning Busan, check the Lotte Giants Baseball schedule and see if you can fit a game in! It's a MUST!

DAY 7: GO TO BUSAN FROM THE TEMPLE STAY ....

A.M.
→ Head to the KTX office at Seoul Station and get your ticket for the train to Busan!
→ Approximately three hours later, check into your hotel in Nampo-dong.
P.M.
→ Collapse and enjoy your hotel
→ Grab a bite to eat at Gaemijip
→ Walk (or taxi) to Jagalchi Fish Market
→ Wander with a beer and prepare to be fascinated
→ Choose whichever little restaurant calls to you and order a fried fish!

DAY 8: NAMPO ....

A.M.
→ Wake up and head straight to Gukje/Nampodong Market
→ After you've shopped, ate and caffeinated, drop off any goodies at your hotel
→ Then jump on a bus to Gamcheon Culture Village -and remember to get your stamps!

P.M.
→ Keep eating at Gwangbokdong Food Street

DAY 9: NAMPO

A.M.
→ Get on the bus to Samgwangsa Temple
→ Walk to Seongok Traditional Market

P.M.
→ Take a bus to Seomyeon's Jeonpo Street
→ Grab caffeine and lunch on Jeonpo Cafe Street (just a walking street with lots to see).
→ Plan on dinner in Seomyeon Food Alley and take in the neighborhood's hipster nightlife.
→ Have a beer at Galmegi Brewing and Thursday Party
→ Take the subway back to Nampo

DAY 10: HAEUNDAE

A.M.
→ Check out of your hotel and head to Haeundae
→ Treat yourself to a nice hotel, it's your last one!

P.M.
→ Wander Haeundae Market
→ Hit the beach (bring snacks and a book)
→ Wander Haeundae some more, popping into Thursday Party and see where the night takes you!

DAY 11: HAEUNDAE

A.M.
→ Go to OBok Restaurant for a traditional Korean breakfast
→ Visit the Sea Life Busan Aquarium
→ Afterwards, take a bus to Haedong Yonggungsa (The Water Temple)

P.M.
→ Collapse at your hotel and get cute
→ Take the subway to Gwangalli Beach
→ Watch the sunset from the beach and enjoy the bridge lighting up!
→ Head to Club MONK around 8pm for dinner wait until 9pm when the live music starts
→ Subway or Taxi back to Haeundae

DAY 12: HAEUNDAE
A.M.
→ Wake up and head straight to Shinsegae Department Store
→ Head to the food court for breakfast and coffee

→ Wander the department store
→ Head to Spa Land inside the Department Store
→ Stay here all day!!!

P.M.
→ Head home and freshen up
→ Go to Wolfhound Pub for dinner and maybe meet some other travelers/ expats

DAY 13: HAEUNDAE

A.M.
→ Check out of your hotel and leave your bags there
→ Take this guided day trip to Tongyeong! ⟶

P.M.
→ Pick up your bags and head to Haeundae Spa Center (you will be sleeping here)
→ Enjoy the spa facilities, eat dinner here, and sleep here!

DAY 14: HOME

→ Wake up and have breakfast at the spa
→ Check out and either head to Gimhae International Airport to fly to Incheon or take the KTX train
→ Give yourself plenty of time to make that connecting flight!

South Korea Notes...

ONE WEEK: *Seoul & Jeju Island*

*ONLY CHOOSE THIS ITINERARY IF YOU ARE COMFORTABLE RENTING A CAR OR SCOOTER TO EXPLORE JEJU ISLAND.

DAY 1: LAND IN SOUTH KOREA

A.M.
→ From the airport, head to your hotel in Hongdae
Shower and collapse

P.M.
→ Hit Hongdae Walking Street immediately!
→ Shop, eat, and live it up tonight! This is your night to let loose.
→ Pass by Tokkijung Project, if there is no line, go there for dinner (if there is a line, go eat all the street food you can find)
→ If you really want to party, go to NB2 nightclub.

DAY 2: SEOUL

A.M.
→ Wake up slowly and hungover
→ Grab a coffee at any Cat Cafe while you revisit this book
→ Hop on a bus and go spend the whole day at Dragon Hill Spa - get massages, scrubs, sleep in the sleeping room, eat - everything!

P.M.
→ Head back home to collapse in your hotel room!
→ Go on a food tour!

DAY 3: SEOUL

A.M.
→ Hop on a bus to Bukchon Hanok Village
→ Walk around and look for a place that rents Hanbok (the traditional Korean dresses and dress-up).
→ Once you're dressed, explore the complex grounds for culture, breakfast and a caffeine pick-me-up

P.M.
→ Put your normal clothes back on and walk 10 minutes to Gyeongbokgung Palace to explore
→ Take a Taxi to Gwanghwamun Jip for dinner - order the Kimchi Stew
→ Walk to Sanchez Makgeolli and try the alcoholic Makgeolli
→ Hop on the Subway back to Hongdae (you're next to Anguk Station)
→ Grab some snacks from 7-Eleven and head back to your hotel for a night in with weird snacks in bed.

DAY 4: TEMPLE STAY
A.M.
→ Head to check into Jingwansa's temple stay program...
→ Spend the night here to relax and reflect

DAY 5: TRAVEL DAY
→ From the Temple Stay, head to the airport for a flight to Jeju Island!
→ Check into your hotel in Jeju City and explore near your hotel for the evening.
→ Rent a car or a scooter

DAY 6: EXPLORING JEJU
A.M.
→ Start with breakfast at Jeju Five-day Folk Market
→ Wander the market and the Folk Village for an hour or two
P.M.
→ Head to Seogwipo and spend a few hours wandering around Jeju's waterfalls.
→ Grab lunch at Seogwipo Maeil Olle Market
→ Spend the evening at Seogwipo's laid-back beach bars

DAY 7: JEJU ISLAND
A.M.
→ Spend your last morning at Dongmun Traditional Market
→ Head to the airport back to Seoul and to your connecting flight home

TWO WEEKS: *Seoul, Gangneung, & Busan*

◊ **WEEK ONE - FOLLOW THE SEOUL ITINERARY ABOVE**

◊ **WEEK TWO - FOLLOW THE ITINERARY BELOW**

DAY 7: TRAVEL DAY

A.M.

→ From the Temple Stay, head to Seoul Station and get on the KTX train to Gangneung!

→ About 2.5 hours later, check into your hotel.

P.M.

→ Wander Gangneung's city center for shopping, nightlife and food!

DAY 8: GANGNEUNG

A.M.

→ Head to Gangneung Coffee Street for a pick-me-up

→ Spend some time enjoying the soft sands and sparkling sea views of Anmok Beach.

P.M.

→ Jump on a bus to Jumunjin Fish Market

→ Spend the day wandering and eating (or eating and wandering)

→ DAY 9: GANGNEUNG

A.M.

→ Head to Gyeongpo Beach for sunrise

→ Then cycle or walk around Gyeongpo Lake

→ Go to Songpo Seafood & Sashimi for brunch

P.M.

→ Head back into the city to check out

→ Take a bus to Busan

→ Check into your hotel in Nampo-dong

→ Collapse and enjoy your hotel

→ Wander outside for some street food

DAY 10: BUSAN

A.M.
→ Wake up and head straight to Gukje/Nampodong Market

P.M.
→ Grab a bite to eat at Gaemijip
→ Walk (or taxi) to Jagalchi Fish Market
→ Wander with a beer and prepare to be fascinated
→ Choose whichever little restaurant calls to you and order a fried fish!

DAY 11: NAMPO

A.M.
→ Take a bus to Seomyeon's Jeonpo Street
→ Grab caffeine and lunch on Jeonpo Cafe Street (just a walking street with lots to see).

P.M.
→ Eat lunch at Seomyeon Food Alley and take in the neighborhood's hipster nightlife.
→ Have a beer at Galmegi Brewing and Thursday Party
→ Take subway line 1 to Nampodong Station
→ Head straight to dinner on Gwangbokdong Food Street
→ Collapse in a food coma

DAY 12: HAEUNDAEAM

A.M.
→ Check out of your hotel and head to Haeundae
→ Treat yourself to a nice hotel, it's your last one!

P.M.
→ Wander Haeundae Market
→ Hit the beach (bring snacks and a book)
→ Wander Haeundae some more, popping into Thursday Party and see where the night takes you!

- or -

DAY 12: HAEUNDAE

A.M.
→ Go to OBok Restaurant for a traditional Korean breakfast
→ Visit the Sea Life Busan Aquarium
→ Afterwards, take a bus to Haedong Yonggungsa (The Water Temple)

P.M.
→ Refresh at your hotel and get cute

→Take the subway to Gwangalli Beach
→Watch the sunset from the beach and enjoy the bridge lighting up!
→Head to Club MONK around 8pm for dinner wait until 9pm when the live music starts
→Subway or Taxi back to Haeundae

DAY 13: HAEUNDAE

A.M.
→Wake up and head straight to Shinsegae Department Store
→Head to the food court for breakfast and coffee
→Wander the department store
→Head to Spa Land inside the Department Store
→Stay here all day!!!

P.M.
→Head home and freshen up
→Go to Wolfhound Pub for dinner and maybe meet some other travelers/expats

DAY 14: HOME

A.M.
→Wake up and have breakfast at the spa
→Check out and either head to Gimhae International Airport to fly to Incheon or take the KTX train
→Give yourself plenty of time to make that connecting flight!
→Then jump on a bus to Gamcheon Culture Village -and remember to get your stamps!

P.M.
→Keep eating at Gwangbokdong Food Street

ONE MONTH: *North to South*

A month leaves you a lot of wiggle room. Instead of giving you a day-to-day itinerary, I'm going to leave you with a bucket list!

SEOUL: 7 DAYS

WHAT TO DO AND SEE...

.... Go on a Food Tour
.... Rent a Hanbok and Explore Bukchon Hanok Village
.... Gyeongbukgong Palace
.... Jogyesa Temple
.... Go on a K-Pop Tour
.... Eat Street Food at Gwangjang Market
.... Wander Myeongdong Street Food Alley
.... Tour the DMZ
.... Go Clubbing in Gangnam and Hongdae
.... Visit a Noraebang
.... Relax at a Jjimjilbang
.... Spend the Night at a Temple Stay
.... Go to Lotte World
.... Hike Mount Bukhansan
.... Shop vintage boutiques in Insa-dong
.... Stock up on skincare products
.... Explore Hongdae Walking Street

GANGNEUNG: 4 DAYS

WHAT TO DO AND SEE...

.... Catch a Festival (spring or fall are the main seasons).
.... Visit Gyeongpo Beach
.... Visit Jeongdongjin Beach
.... Visit Anmok Beach and Coffee Street

.... Eat sundubu-jjigae at Chodang Tofu Village
.... Watch the Sunrise at Sculpture Park
.... Walk on the Jeongdongjin glass-bottomed bridge
.... Try gamjajeon (potato pancakes)
.... Visit Chamsori Gramophone Museum and Edison Science Museum
.... Visit Ojukheon House

GYOENGJU: 5 DAYS
WHAT TO DO AND SEE...
.... Yangdong Village
.... Try Gyochon Hanok Village to try beopju
.... Hike Mount Namsan
.... Gyeongju National Park
.... Anapji (Wolji) Pond/Woljeonggyo Bridge
.... Try Hwangnam bread
.... Gyeongju World
.... Relax at Bomun Lake
.... Daereungwon Tumuli Park
.... Gyeongju Bird Park
.... Participate in a tea ceremony at Bulguksa Temple
.... Stay overnight at Golgulsa Temple
.... Donggung Palace
.... Seokguram Grotto
.... Cheomseongdae
.... King Munmu's Underwater Tomb

BUSAN: 7 DAYS
WHAT TO DO AND SEE...
.... Jagalchi Fish Market
.... Wander Nampo-dong
.... Hike Geumnyeongsan Mountain, Igidae Park, or Seunghaksan Mountain
.... Drink at Thursday Party
.... Catch the Busan International Film Festival if you're there in October.
.... Spend a day at Spa Land
.... Go beach-hopping: Haeundae, Gwangali, Songdo, and Dadaepo.
.... Haedong Yonggungsa (The Water Temple)
.... Seokbulsa Temple

.... Geumjeongsanseong Fortress
.... Samgwangsa Temple
.... Gamcheon Culture Village
.... Sea Life Busan Aquarium

GEOJE/OEDO: 2 DAYS

WHAT TO DO AND SEE...

.... Watch the Sunset on Windy Hill
.... Go to the Deokpo Beach Penguin Swim Festival in January
.... Climb Mount Gyeryongsan
.... Hakdong Pebble Beach
.... Gujora Beach
.... Oedo Botanical Garden
.... Party in Okpo

JEJU ISLAND: 5 DAYS

WHAT TO DO AND SEE...

.... Hit the beaches: Iho Taewoo Beach, Hamdeok Beach, Gwakji Beach,
.... Hyeopjae Beach, Jungmun Beach, Hado Beach
.... Watch haenyeo (sea women) dive for seafood
.... Explore Waterfalls: Jeongbang, Cheonjiyeon, Cheonjeyeon,
Wonang Falls
.... Go for Breathtaking Hikes: Hallasan, Seongsan Ilchul-bong (Sunrise
Peak), Jeju Olle Walking Trails, and Suwolbong Peak
.... Dine on Abalone and Black Pork
.... Seonimgo Bridge
.... Jeju Folk Village
.... Hallim Park
.... Explore Manjanggul Cave

Bonus Chapter!

—

Teaching English in South Korea

—

So, it happened...

You fell in love and now you want to stay in South Korea while making some cash, living for free, and playing with cute Korean kids day in and day out. Girl, I get it! South Korea has a unique way of sneaking into your heart.

If you just have to spend more time in this incredible country, you're in luck - English teachers are pretty much always in demand here. Teaching in South Korea certainly won't make you a million dollars, but you'll walk away infinitely richer in travel, friends, and unforgettable experiences. Plus, many teachers are able to pay off their student loans or credit cards while they're here.

For some insider tips on what teaching in South Korea is really like, plus how to find a teaching job and where to travel in your spare time, read on!

Yep, that's me!

Psst. I wrote the most comprehensive teaching guide ever for South Korea. It's on my blog here...

How to Find a Teaching Job in South Korea

Public schools, private schools (hagwons), after school programs, even universities - there are tons of places to teach in South Korea! Some big companies even hire English teachers to tutor their staff.

But not all teaching jobs are created equal. Some will offer you comfortable working hours, decent salary and benefits, and plenty of time off. Others will have you stuck working long hours for little pay, leaving little time or money to explore the country. You'll want to do your research and not just jump into the first job you find!

I'll talk some more about how to find the right job, one that will pay you well and give you plenty of time for fun, but first – do you qualify to teach in South Korea?

REQUIREMENTS TO TEACH ENGLISH IN SOUTH KOREA

◆Be a native English speaker from a recognized English-speaking country (the United States, the United Kingdom, Ireland, New Zealand, South Africa, or Australia).

◆Have a bachelor's degree from an accredited university. It doesn't have to be in education; any bachelor's degree is fine. I was able to land a job with a Sociology degree. Clear criminal record check. Don't worry about little things like speeding tickets; they're looking for bigger charges, like DUIs or misdemeanors (my blog will walk you through the criminal records check).

◆Get your teaching certification. Most teaching jobs in South Korea require a TEFL, TESOL, or CELTA certificate with 100 or more course hours. If you're looking to teach in a private school, you should be okay getting the accreditation online, but some public schools require a certain number of hours in a live classroom. Again, check my blog about teaching in South Korea at Alexa-West.com

TYPES OF TEACHING JOBS

When you start looking for English teacher jobs in South Korea, most of what you find will fall into one of three categories.

◊ Public School Jobs

Public school teaching gigs are among the cushiest. Public school jobs typically have set hours (think 9-5) with limits on how many hours per week you can work. In terms of benefits, you'll get:

→ An allowance to help you get settled

→ Free furnished housing or a housing stipend

severance pay

→ Allowance for travel into and out of the country / the school pays for your flight

→ Health insurance

→ All national holidays off, plus as much as 18 days paid vacation.

Most public-school teaching jobs are in elementary schools, although you can sometimes find a job in middle schools or high schools. You'll have a Korean co-teacher with you in the classroom as well, meaning you get to split the workload. But this co-teacher thang does come with its own cultural challenges.

Competition for public school teaching jobs is fierce, so if you have your heart set on working in this environment, start looking and applying for jobs as far as six months out!

◊ Private School (hagwon) Jobs

Most English teachers, particularly first-timers, find themselves in the hagwon system. Each hagwon is independently run so the exact environment and job details will vary. Generally speaking, though, you'll work more hours per week and get fewer vacation days as a teacher in a hagwon. However, these private schools have faster hiring times and tend to pay better than public school jobs.

You likely won't have a co-teacher if you're working in a hagwon. And the teaching hours can be a little odd; if you work with the younger grades, you'll likely teach in the mornings but if you're working with middle school or high school students, you'll teach at night, after their normal class day has ended.

I taught in hagwons. I preferred their hours and pay. I taught at one school in Busan and one school in Daegu. If you want to pick my brain, message me on Instagram @SoloGirlsTravelGuide.

Pro Tip: There is a "Korean Green List" (google it) and "Black List" of hagwon schools in South Korea. Just search the school's name to which you're applying and see if it was dramatic enough to land on either list.

◊ University Jobs

If you can land a teaching job in a university in South Korea, you've hit the jackpot! Higher salaries, fewer working hours, more freedom . . . the real dream! The downside is that these can be difficult to find, and you'll likely need a master's degree and some previous teaching experience to get it.

How do most teachers land a university job? They apply for the Master's program at that University, study abroad (usually an education degree) and are then offered a gig when they finish.

Fun Fact: University Teachers in South Korea are given the distinguished title of "Professor" even if they're not qualified professors by US standards.

Pro Tip: You will occasionally see private tutoring jobs advertised, but those are actually illegal in South Korea for holders of an E-2 visa (what most teachers get). If you have this type of visa, don't take the chance! Just stick to the school jobs.

Fun Fact: You are one year older in South Korea! Koreans consider the time a person spends in the womb to be the first year of their life, so babies turn one when they're born.

◊ **Option 1:** Apply with EPIK (the public school system). For public school jobs, you'll need to go through an official government program; check out the EPIK (English Program in Korea; www.epik.go.kr).

◊ **Option 2:** Use a recruiter. Recruiters work for larger agencies that match schools with teachers. Not only can they help you with the job search itself, they generally have a feel for the school you're applying to and can advise as to whether it'll be the right fit. They can also help you negotiate your contract so everything that should be included, is.

Adventure Teaching (www.adventureteaching.com) and Gone2Korea (www.gone2korea.com) are two good recruiting companies to start with.

Pro Tip: Choose one recruiter and stick with them! If you work with multiple recruiters, your resume can get submitted multiple times to the same position - not a professional look, and one that can send you straight to the bottom of the list!

◊ **Option 3:** Search Dave's ESL Café to find a job posting you like...then contact the recruiter or school representing this post (this is how I found my jobs...but it takes some leg-work).

Dave's ESL Cafe (http://www.eslcafe.com/jobs/korea/) has been around since the 90s and remains the most popular place to search for jobs.

◊ **Option 4:** Pick the exact school you like and message them. If you're looking for university jobs, check the university website itself, since most will post open positions directly.

To apply to any teaching position, you'll need to have a resume, cover letter, and photo. Make sure to include your nationality and English-speaking ability at the top of your resume. Having all of these things on hand and

Teaching Scams to Watch Out For

Let's face it, picking up your entire life and moving across the world is huge. You need to make sure you're doing it right, watching out for yourself, and not getting taken advantage of. While scammers aren't wildly common in the world of overseas teaching, you do still run across a bad apple here and there, from sleazy recruiters to bad employers.

Here are a few red flags to look out for when looking for a teaching job in South Korea.

◊ Recruiters Who Want Money

A recruiter who's the real deal gets paid by the school, not the applicants. If a recruiter wants to charge you a fee for helping with your search, that is 100% a scam. Run for the hills.

◊ Fake Positions/Schools

When you find a position you like, head straight to Google. Most schools these days have some kind of online presence, whether it's a full website or just a Facebook page. If you can't find anything about the school at all, or if the site seems to be full of vague information and stock photos, it's time to move on.

Pro Tip: If the job posting asks you to email your resume and information to someone, check into that email address! This is doubly important if it's a generic email, like Gmail or Hotmail. Go to the school website and see if it matches any of the contact information listed there. If it doesn't, you can always reach out to the school's official email address to confirm that the position is real.

It's hard to tell whether a school will turn out to be a good employer or a bad one before you actually get to Korea, but if an employer has an excessive number of negative reviews, that's a sign to proceed with caution.

Teaching Culture

What should you expect when you become a teacher in South Korea? Obviously, your life will look different depending on where you end up teaching, but there you will find some common themes in expat and teacher life!

✔ **Your students will love you.** Like, really love you. Be prepared for ear-to-ear smiles and constant hugs and touching, especially if you're working with younger kids. If you're blonde, have curly hair, are really tall, are not white, have visible tattoos . . . basically if anything about you is not commonly seen in Asia, they'll be even more fascinated.

Pro Tip: Watch out for ddong chim - the Asian wedgie. This is when kids will literally try to stick their fingers up your butt. I'm serious - it's a thing. They'll stop after a few times of you swatting their hand away and discussing the meaning of the word "inappropriate," but it's definitely something you need to be prepared for.

✔ **Making friends will happen organically.** No need to worry about being lonely when you're a teacher! You'll most likely end up in a city with a ton of other teachers and expats, and friendships form really quickly because you're all in the same boat - trying to acclimate to the crazy/beautiful world that is South Korea. Most young Koreans are also eager to befriend westerners, so you'll end up with a big international squad!

✔ **Be prepared for tight living quarters.** In general, houses in South Korea are smaller than you're probably used to. That's even more the case when you're living in teacher housing (or on a teacher's stipend). Many teachers end up in studio apartments with kind of bare-bones amenities and not a lot of extra space. But hey, you're not in Korea to hang out at home!

✔ **South Korean drinking culture is no joke.** Speaking of not being at home . . . let's talk about Korean drinking culture. When South Koreans go out, they go out hard. Team-building nights are very common for Korean employees, and they often involve multiple stages of eating and drinking, wrapping up at a noraebang. Think getting home at 2am. In addition, lots of expat life centers around nightlife as well.

That being said, if you're not a big drinker, don't despair! Your colleagues will respect it if you say that you don't drink, and there's so much else to do in Korea!

✔ **Yes, you can save money!** Again, this will differ depending on where you're teaching, but you should expect to make around $2,000-2,500 a month. That might not sound like much but remember, your housing will be taken care of! It's totally possible to save a decent chunk of your money, either for travel adventures or actual savings, if you embrace certain lifestyle choices. This means eating Korean food (western food can be incredibly expensive in Korean grocery stores), cooking at home sometimes, taking advantage of it if your school provides free lunch, searching flight and travel deals, and not going crazy with the shopping.

Teaching Notes...

....

....

....

....

....

Best Cities to Teach English

Depending on the job market, you might not have a ton of freedom to choose where you want to teach. But if you do find yourself with some options, here are some of my top picks for South Korean cities to teach in!

SEOUL

Kind of a no-brainer, right? Why wouldn't you want to live and work in South Korea's most dynamic city? The expat community in Seoul is enormous, so you'll have no problem making friends. And of course, there's always something to do! From nightlife to festivals, it's basically impossible to be bored in Seoul.

Of course, there are a couple downsides to teaching in Seoul. First, the city is massive, so if you don't end up living near your school or your friends, you'll spend a lot of time commuting. Second, you'll have to deal with constant crowds and packed public transportation. And finally, sometimes it can be hard to get any real "downtime" in such an exciting, active city; if you're the kind of person who needs a quiet night here or there, the next two options might be more your speed!

SEOUL OUTSKIRTS

If you like the idea of experiencing everything Seoul has to offer but still being able to get your eight hours of beauty sleep on a regular basis, consider the city's suburbs! Places like Suwon, Ilsan, and Anyang are all super convenient to the city but offer a much calmer, quieter lifestyle. They each have their own long list of things to do and explore, and you can get into Seoul proper easily in about an hour.

INCHEON

Incheon is another great option if you want to be near Seoul but don't want the uber-big city life. It's located between Seoul and South Korea's biggest international airport, making it quick and easy to hop on a plane for a weekend in Japan or China. And for when you just need a night out in the big city, Incheon is also connected directly to Seoul by subway.

BUSAN

Busan was the first city I ever lived in South Korea...actually, it was the first city I ever lived in in Asia! It was such a fantastic place to slowly integrate into Asian culture. It's absolutely Korean but with a layer of foreigner-friendly culture that made it easy to navigate, integrate and make friends. Plus, it's gorgeous and you'll never run out of things to do.

Bonus - The beaches!

DAEGU

Here is my favorite teacher city- where I spent 1 amazing year at Kid's College. Daegu is one of South Korea's best-kept teacher secrets! It's a mid-sized city so you'll get all the amenities of city life without Seoul's constant craziness. Daegu is also much more compact and walkable than Seoul, making it easy to meet up with your friends for a night out without spending a ton of time on a bus.

GEOJE

For a truly one-of-a-kind living experience, head south to Geoje Island. This island west of Busan has just about everything you would want from island life - sandy beaches, sparkling blue water, subtropical climate, tons of hiking and outdoor activities, plus a fun nightlife scene. The island is home to one of the world's largest shipyards, meaning there is a huge yet close-knit community of expats. Geoje is connected to Busan by bridge and undersea tunnel (so cool!) so you can get to the mainland in about an hour.

One con to Geoje is that the cost of living is higher on the island than on the mainland. You'll need to take that into consideration when planning your budget.

In case you need that extra push, just let me tell you…teaching in South Korea was the best decision I ever made for myself.

Fun Fact: Taekwondo was born in South Korea 2,000 years ago.

Resources
for South Korea

Medical, Gynecology Services & Female Stuff

For everything reproductive health including birth control & IUDs, STD testing, pap smears, ultrasounds, and more. You'll find that OBGYN services in South Korea are fantastic. I'm talking PAP smear for $40.

QUICK LIST OF RECOMMENDED OBGYNS

SEOUL

Songpa GOEUNBIT Women's Clinic

They speak English. They offer every service you need, including IUD placements, STD testing and PAP smears - they even do COVID testing and vaccinations.

- **Contact:** 010 9608 3985
- **Email:** goeunbit2021@gmail.com
- **Kakao Talk ID:** goeunbit
- **Address:** J 95 Ogeum-ro, Songpa-gu

BUSAN

Dr. Kim Jeeyeon's Gynecology & Obstetrics

She speaks English and is the go-to OBGYN for many expats. She offers all OBGYN services including helping you select birth control.

- **Contact:** 051-529-9167
- **Email:** yeonik20@hotmail.com
- **Address:** 268-19 Suan-dong, Dongnae-gu, Busan, South Korea

Learn more:

JEJU

Jeju (Cheju) Halla Hospital

For an island hospital, this place really has it's shit together! They provide all the services above and specialize in "one-stop support center for victims of sexual violence".

- **Address:** 65 Doryeong-ro, Yeon-dong

Learn more:

South Korea Packing List

First, don't stress. Korea is the land of shopping! As long as you have your passport, bank card and a decent backpack, you're ready for South Korea. No matter what you do or don't pack - you'll be just fine. Anything you need or forget, you can buy here.

As always, my best packing advice is this: don't overdo it!

Pack light, especially if you're hopping from city to city. As you'll see in a moment, I highly recommend traveling with a backpack instead of a roller suitcase for optimal city-hopping.

As you pack, think about the weather, particularly if you're coming in winter. For winter months, bring a couple Long-sleeve tees (thermal are best), a couple of heavier sweaters, and a warm coat. Buy your scarves, hats and gloves here!

After living in South Korea for two years in different regions of the country, here are my ultimate suggestions on what to pack!

THE LOGISTICS

✔ PASSPORT WITH AT LEAST 6 MONTHS VALIDITY

Some countries enforce it and some countries don't – but to play it safe, you need to have at least 6 months validity on your passport. For example, if it's January 1st, 2024, and your passport expires before June 1st, 2024, they might not let you in the country and you'll have to return home immediately.

✔ TRAVEL INSURANCE

Yes, you do need it. Everything from minor bouts of food poisoning to helicopter medevac off a mountain, a standard travel insurance policy is a non-negotiable in my (literal) book.

Check your current medical insurance plan. They might already cover Indonesia. If they don't, here is what I use:

 ◊ World Nomads which offers full-coverage plans for extremely reasonable prices.

◊ Safetywing is also a really affordable option, especially if you're traveling long term.

✔ EMERGENCY MONEY SOURCE / $100 CASH US

Have a secret stash of cash and a backup credit card in case you get in a sticky situation. Keep this emergency money source separate from your other cards and cash so that if you lose your wallet, you won't lose the secret stash, too

✔ THE CORRECT CREDIT AND DEBIT CARDS

Generally speaking, you can use your debit and credit cards just about everywhere in South Korea (although I definitely recommend pulling out some cash when you land for street vendors).

But please take the time to get the correct travel-friendly cards before you fly. They will save you money and provide you extra travel insurance as you travel.

As a rule of thumb: Travel with two debit cards and at least one credit card. – either 2 debit cards or 1 debit + 1 credit. That way, even if something happens to your debit card or credit card, you'll still be able to move around the country and get yourself home.

The cards you need are here...

✔ THE PERFECT BACKPACK OR SUITCASE

In South Korea, you'll be taking planes, trains and taxis to get around. You don't want to be lugging a roller suitcase with you. Instead, carry a traveler's backpack.

 ◊ I recommend a hard case, carry-on size spinner like this one.

However, I will be a backpack girl til the day I die – no matter how smooth the roads are.

◊ The Bag I Recommend...The Osprey Farpoint 40 Litre Backpack:

It's been over 5 years that I've been using this bag. I love it so much that I just bought the exact same model again to use for another 5 years.

   ◊ This bag qualifies as a carry-on

   ◊ It's extremely comfortable to wear

   ◊ The open-zip style means that you can keep your clothes organized

   ◊ I swear it's got Mary Poppins magic because I can fit 3 months of clothes in one tiny space

THE ESSENTIALS

✔ UNIVERSAL PLUG ADAPTER

South Korea uses 220 voltage (as opposed to the standard 110v used in the U.S.). You're generally okay to plug in the basics, like your phone charger. But if you have anything that can't handle 220 voltage or anything with a three-pronged plug, like some laptops, you'll need a universal adapter. Pick up a cheap one from REI, Target, and Amazon.

✔ QUICK-DRY TOWEL

Hostel girls! Hostels usually don't provide towels so it's nice to bring a travel towel of your own. Not all hostels provide towels, so this is a good way to save a few extra bucks instead of paying a fee to rent one. A microfiber towel is nice to have, especially during the rainy season when the heat isn't there to dry things quickly. Plus, it can double as your beach towel!

....

✔ TRAVEL UMBRELLA AND RAINCOAT

If you plan to be in South Korea from July through September, you will 100% need some rain gear! Be prepared for at least a day or two of wet weather during your stay.

Get a compact umbrella like this ☞

And a lightweight rain coat, one that is actually waterproof, like this ☞

....

✔ MENSTRUAL CUP OR TAMPONS

You can find tampons in South Korean pharmacies and convenience stores but if you're particular about your brand, it's better to just bring your own.

I started using a menstrual cup last year and will never go back to tampons!

You're going to be in a bathing suit on the beach and out on the water! And if you've never used a menstrual cup, they are a game changer. Save money every month, go 12 hours with no leaks & swim with no drips.

The one I use is called Saalt. Get it here ☞

....

✔ WALKING SHOES

You'll be walking a LOT in South Korea, even if you aren't hiking up a mountain! So, bring shoes that will be comfortable for a long day on your feet, as well as shoes that are easy to slip on and off.

Bring 3 pairs of shoes:

◊ 1 Pair of Flip Flops or Slides

◊ 1 Pair of Cute Walking Sandals

◊ 1 Pair of Hiking / Running Shoes

This is my official trifecta of shoes. Through rain, up mountains, and on long sweaty walks, they've never failed me. I replace the same pairs of shoes every year – find them in my travel store.

✔ PASHMINA / WRAP FOR VISITING TEMPLES

If you're in South Korea during the summer months, you'll likely be going sleeveless a large part of the time. Be culturally sensitive and throw a pashmina or a light wrap into your purse to toss over your shoulders when visiting temples or shrines.

I have a fabulous wrap in my travel store on my website that doubles as a blanket!

✔ TRAVEL CHARGER

From Naver Translate to Naver Maps, you'll be using your phone a ton. Carry a portable charger with you to make sure you're never caught without battery life. There's nothing worse than watching your phone die and realizing you don't know how to get back to your hotel!

✔ HUMIDITY-PROOF MAKEUP (SUMMER); MOISTURIZER AND LIP BALM (YEAR-ROUND)

South Korea's weather can be a challenge for your skincare routine, so be prepared! From greasy foundation and running mascara in the summer to scaly, red cheeks in the winter, you need back-up! I say, bring a couple of your makeup essentials but plan to go makeup shopping at stores like Etude House or Innisfree when you arrive!

Clean, Hole-Free Socks and Nail Clippers (maybe even some nail polish)

In Korea, the state of your feet matter. Chances are, you'll be going barefoot at least once or twice on your trip. So, make sure your feet look the part! Make sure your socks are clean and without holes (don't bring your favorite old pair!) and your toe nails are trimmed (and painted, if that's your thing). It's a respect thang.

✔ EMPTY SPACE IN YOUR BAG

It took me 5 years to learn that the less stuff you have, the more free you are. You are free to pick up and move around, free to shop for souvenirs, and free from relying on porters and taxis to help you carry your luggage. Plus, you're going to need space for all that extra shopping over here.

WHAT NOT TO PACK

✗ Tons of Skincare - Korea is the skincare capital of the world and you'll want a reason to shop!

✗ High-heels (with all the walking you'll be doing, high heels don't make sense but wedges are okay).

✗ A Curling Iron in the summer (with this humidity...no point)

✗ Sunscreen. South Korean women are obsessive about protecting their skin, so you can find excellent sunscreen products at pharmacies and convenience stores! Just make sure not to grab one that doubles as a bleaching product.

Bringing Medication to South Korea

South Korea takes drug use very seriously and they have some strict limitations when it comes to medicines and ingredients that you can bring into the country.

Prohibited OTC medicines:

→ CBD oil/gummies and hemp-derivative products

→ Any medicine containing Codeine

Other OTC medicines:

You can bring up to a 60-day supply of any non-prohibited OTC medicine, including vitamins.

Prohibited prescription medications:

→ Opium

→ Cannabis

→ Amphetamines/methamphetamines, including medications for the treatment of ADD/ADHD (Adderall, Vyvanse, Dexedrine)

→ Any narcotic

Other prescription medications:

For prescriptions that don't contain narcotics or amphetamines, you can bring up to six bottles (or the equivalent to a three-month supply). You'll need to bring the original prescriptions, a letter from your doctor specifying the medical condition the medicine is used for, and a statement from your doctor specifying which medicines you will be carrying. Keep all medications in their original bottle.

Locally Available Medications:

South Korea has a ton of pharmacies in major cities so if you come down with a cold, headache, or sore throat, you can find treatment here. The brands and active ingredients may differ but you can use Naver Translate to communicate with the pharmacist and find what you need!

Note: If you are coming to South Korea as a teacher, congratulations - you have medical insurance and access to some amazing doctors and hospitals who can help you sort out your medications!

☎ HOW TO CALL KOREAN NUMBERS FROM A FOREIGN (OUTSIDE KOREA) NUMBER

Let's say you're given this number

02 2086 4600

If you just type that number in your phone, it might not work.

Solution: drop the *0* and add the country code *(+82)*

So now the number looks like this:

+82 2 2086 4600

Ps. That's the number of my Botox guy, Sergio. Might as well just save that right now.

MINI
Directory
FOR SOUTH KOREA

THE ESSENTIALS

Fire and Ambulance:
Dial 119

Emergency Medical Information Center (24/7):
Dial 1339

Police:
Dial 112

Korea Travel Helpline (multi-lingual, 24/7):
Dial 1330 - use this for translation services!

International Emergency Rescue (Seoul):
+82 02 790 7561

Lost and Found Center (Seoul):
+82 2 182

....

APPLE PHONE REPAIR
Apple Garosugil
46 Apgujeong-ro 12-gil, Sinsa-dong, Seoul
+82 2 2086 4600

HOSPITALS

SEOUL

Seoul Asan Medical Center

☐ + 82 2 3010 5001 (English)

🏥 88, Olympic-ro 43-gil, Songpa-gu, Seoul

Sinchon Severance Hospital

+82 2 2228 5800 (English)

🏥 50-1, Yonsei-ro, Seodaemun-gu, Seoul

Samsung Medical Center

☐ +82 2 3410 0200 (English)

🏥 81, Irwon-ro, Gangnam-gu, Seoul

Seoul National University Hospital ☐ +82 2 2072 0505 (English)

🏥 101, Daehak-ro, Jongno-gu, Seoul

The Catholic University of Korea Seoul St. Mary's Hospital

☐ +82 2 2258 5745 (English)

🏥 222, Banpo-daero, Seocho-gu, Seoul

BUSAN

Inje University Paik Hospital

☐ +82 51 797 0566 (English)

🏥 875, Haeun-daero, Haeundae-gu, Busan

Pro Tip: Not all Korean hospitals accept credit cards, so if you need to check into a hospital, make sure you have at least $50 cash.

EMBASSIES

British Embassy

🏥 24 Sejong-daero 19-gil, Jeong-dong, Jung-gu, Seoul

☐ Emergency number: +82 2 3210 5500

American Embassy

🏥 188 Sejong-daero, Sejongno, Jongno-gu, Seoul

☐ Emergency numbers: +82 2 397 4114 (9am-5pm); after hours +82 2 397 4114

Canadian Embassy

🏥 21 Jeongdong-gil, Jeong-dong, Jung-gu, Seoul

☐ Emergency number: +82 2 3783 6000

Australian Embassy

🏥 1 Jong-ro, Jongno 1(il)-ga, Jongno-gu, Seoul

☐ Emergency number: +82 2 2003 0100

Always remember...

THAT YOU ARE BRAVER THAN YOU THINK,

STRONGER THAN YOU KNOW,

AND SMARTER THAN YOU BELIEVE.

To every girl who has messaged me or left me a review telling me how these books have impacted you – thank you for
reminding me that travel changes people,
that these books change people.

I love you all!
Women supporting women is how magic happens.

DID YOU LEAVE A REVIEW?

As a self-published author – doing this whole publishing thing by myself – reviews are what keeps The Solo Girl's Travel Guide growing.

If you found my guidebook to be helpful, please leave me a review on Amazon.com

Your review helps other girls find this book and experience a truly life-changing trip.

Ps. I read every single review.

The true story of how
the Solo Girl's Travel Guide
was born...

I was robbed in Cambodia.

Sure, the robber was a child and yes, I might have drunkenly put my purse down in the sand while flirting with an irresistible Swedish boy...but that doesn't change the fact that I found myself without cash, a debit card and hotel key at 1am in a foreign country.

My mini robbery, however, doesn't even begin to compare to my other travel misadventures. I've also been scammed to tears by taxi drivers, idiotically taken ecstasy in a country with the death penalty for drugs and missed my flight because how was I supposed to know that there are two international airports in Bangkok?

It's not that I'm a total idiot.
It's just that...people aren't born savvy travelers.

I'm not talking about hedonistic vacationers who spend their weekend at a resort sipping Mai Tais. I'm talking about train-taking, market-shopping, street food-eating travelers!

Traveling is not second (or third or fourth) nature; it's a skill that only comes with sweaty on-the-ground experience...especially for women!

In the beginning of my travels (aka the first 5 years), I made oodles of travel mistakes. And thank god I did. These mistakes eventually turned me into the resourceful, respected and established travel guru that I am today.

A travel guru that was spawned through a series of being lost, hospitalized, embarrassed, and broke enough times to finally start learning from (and applying) her lessons.

Year-after-year and country-after-country, I started learning things like…

✓ Always check your hostel mattress for bed bugs.

✓ Local alcohol is usually toxic and will give you a hangover that lasts for days.

✓ The world isn't "touristy" once you stop traveling like a tourist.

✓ And most importantly, the best noodle shops are always hidden in back alleys.

After nearly 11 years of traveling solo around the world (4 continents and 26 countries, but who's counting?) – I travel like a gosh darn pro. I save money, sleep better, haggle harder, fly fancier, and speak foreign languages that help me almost almost blend in with the locals despite my blonde hair.

Yeah yeah yeah. I guess it's cool being a travel icon. But shoot…

Do you know how much money, how many panic attacks, and how many life-threatening risks I could have saved and/or avoided if only someone had freakin' queued me into all of this precious information along the way? A lot. A lotta' lot.

So, why didn't I just pick up a travel guide and start educating myself like an adult? I had options…right? I could've bought a copy of Lonely Planet… but how the hell am I supposed to smuggle a 5-pound brick in my carry-on bag? Or DK Eyewitness, perhaps? Hell no. I don't have 8 hours to sift through an encyclopedia and decode details relevant to my solo adventure.

There was no travel guide that would have spared my tears or showed me how to travel safer and smarter.

The book I needed didn't exist. So, I freakin' wrote it myself.

What travel guide do you need me to write next?
Tell me on Instagram ❤ @SoloGirlsTravelGuide

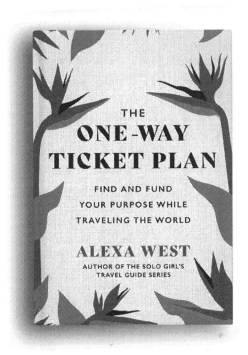

WHERE NEXT?

BALI

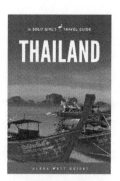
THAILAND

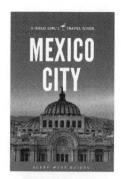
MEXICO CITY

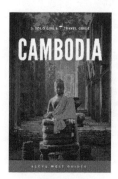
CAMBODIA

JAPAN

VIETNAM

AND MORE...
GET THE WHOLE COLLECTION.

LOVE THIS BOOK?
Please leave us a review!

As a self-published author –
doing this whole publishing thing by myself –
reviews are what keeps
The Solo Girl's Travel Guide growing.

Your review helps other girls find this book
and experience a truly life-changing trip.

Ps. We read every single review.

Room for improvement?
Please email us and tell us how we can make this
book even better!

✉ hello@thesologirlstravelguide.com

PASS IT ON!

This guide book is meant to change lives.
Don't let it sit on a shelf forever and ever.

Before you give this book to a friend
who needs a travel push
or before you leave it in the hostel
for the next travel girl to find…

On the back cover,

✧ write your name,

✧ your Instagram,

✧ and the dates you traveled.

This is your legacy, too.

Oh and when you have inherited this book from a travel
sister, take a picture! I'm dying to see it.

xoxo, Alexa